AUTHORITY

SECRETS FOR ULTIMATE FULFILLMENT IN LIFE

TIMOTHY J. SABO

Study Series

emerge
publishing

TULSA, OKLAHOMA

AUTHORITY
©2023 Timothy J. Sabo

Published by:

Emerge Publishing, LLC
9521B Riverside Parkway, Suite 243
Tulsa, Oklahoma 74137
Phone: 888.407.4447
www.EmergePublishing.com

Author information contact :
Timothy J. Sabo Ministries, Inc.
5223 87 Street Edmonton, Alberta, Canada T6E 5L5
www.triumphantchurch.ca

Library of Congress Cataloging-In-Publication Data

ISBN: 978-1-954966-33-8 Paperback
ISBN: Digital/E-book available on Kindle

BISAC Category:
REL006680 RELIGION / Biblical Reference / Handbooks
REL079000 RELIGION / Christianity / Pentecostal & Charismatic

Printed in Canada

Contents

AUTHORITY

THE MOUNTAIN

When mountain walls confront thy way,
   Why sit and weep? Arise and say,
"Be thou removed!" and they shall be,
   By power of God, cast in the sea.

All power on earth, all power in heaven,
   To Christ, the Son of God, is given;
And from the throne He will endue,
   And hindrances shall flee from you.

O'er all the power of fiend or man,
   Say through the Lord, "I surely can!"
Take from Him power on earth to tread
   On serpent's sting, on dragon's head.

Whate'er thou art, O mountain high,
   Where'er thou art, in earth or sky,
Whene'er thou art, truth is the same:
   "Be thou removed, in Jesus' name!"

"Be thou removed!" Faith bids thee start;
For yonder sea—Arise! Depart!
I may, I can, I must, I will,
The purpose of my God fulfill.

Anonymous

IT'S TIME TO TALK BACK!

"TIM, I HAD A DREAM about you last night!" Those words still resonate in me, taking me back to my Bible college days.

Black Friday in America means a day of serious shopping and, for many, the start of the Christmas season. However, for Edmonton, Alberta, Canada, where I grew up, the term *Black Friday* means a day of serious disaster, marring the history of July 31, 1987, forever.

Several months earlier, when my brother Dean and I were attending Rhema Bible College in Tulsa, Oklahoma, Dean, who had decided to get his pilot's license, flew up to Canada with his buddy Ken from school. They both needed to get some extra flying hours in, so Dean took Ken up to Edmonton in a single-engine plane. When they arrived, my mom and dad picked them up from the airport and drove them out to our farm located at the southern tip of the city. They happily gave Ken a tour of the property, and then he and Dean flew back to Tulsa.

A few weeks later, I met up with Ken in the hallway at school, and the first thing he said to me was, "Tim, I had a dream about you last night!"

I looked at him skeptically. "Ken, what could you actually dream?"

"I dreamt that there was this massive tornado barreling down your big field and heading right towards the barn. It blew the barn away, and then it was coming straight for your house! We all ran into the basement, but it took the house right off the foundation."

"What did you do then?" I asked him.

Without hesitation, he answered, "I rebuked it in Jesus' Name!"

"Ha! Well, I'm telling you that you don't know how to dream. We don't even have tornadoes in Edmonton!" And then I added, "You know, I rebuke it in Jesus' Name too. This dream will not come to pass!"

Life went on. I finished up Bible school at Rhema and headed home for the summer. Late in July, I was with my uncle at a pipeline located directly north of my home, about two miles. Alberta had been experiencing hot and humid weather all week long, triggering a series of strong thunderstorms. But something was different about July 31; the air felt different. Later, we learned that a cold front was blowing in from the neighboring province, causing a low-pressure system. All morning long and into the afternoon, Weather radio Canada issued severe weather watches, but no one really paid attention to them. After all, it was July, and it had been a hot month. However, by early afternoon, the sky had turned a menacing shade of black, and the weather warning upgraded to a severe storm watch.

Now, remember, up to that point, we never got tornadoes in Edmonton, and I didn't know much about them. As I was working with my uncle, the sky suddenly turned black and foreboding. It wasn't long until Weather radio updated the warning; by 3:04 p.m., it again upgraded, this time to a tornado alert. Edmonton and its residents would never be the same.

Subsequently, I found out that our neighbor, who rented the property across the creek to the west of our farm, saw the tornado touch down on the south end of our big field and head straight for the barn. Just before it reached the gully in front of the barn, the tornado suddenly stopped and shifted directions. Turning east, it jumped the highway that butted up to our property, where it picked up momentum and continued on its deadly path of destruction.

By the time Black Friday, July 31, 1987, was over, the damage assessed from this F4 multi-vortex tornado was extensive. It had remained on the ground for over an hour, cutting a swath of ruin almost twenty miles long. As it grew in strength, it reportedly moved throughout rural areas, tossing farm equipment and granaries in the air. It tore through a train yard, ripping up huge train cars, and it barreled through numerous oil refineries, leveling many of the industrial building and tossing many large oil tanks and semi-trailers several blocks away. Persisting northeast and causing severe damage to several neighborhoods, the tornado finally arrived at Evergreen Mobile Home Park. There it wreaked havoc through a seven-hundred-and-fifty-unit trailer park, destroying nearly two hundred homes and leveling them to the ground.

At the end of the day, this twister left twenty-seven people dead, six hundred more injured, more than three hundred homes utterly destroyed, and over three hundred and thirty-three million dollars in property damage. We later learned that this was one of seven tornadoes to hit central Alberta the same day, but praise God, not one of them even touched our property. Ken and I had taken authority over tornadoes months before, rebuking them in Jesus' Name.

When I went back to school in the fall, I brought the front page of the *Edmonton Journal,* showing the news about the tornado. Ken and I praised God together, saying, "It's a good thing that we rebuked it!" I know that our property and lives were saved from imminent destruction that day because we took authority over it months before. Praise God, we have authority over the weather! We can take our example from Jesus who, with storm raging all around, stood up in the boat with His disciples. He was not intimidated by those natural elements but instead declared with boldness, "Peace! Be still!" He had the utmost confidence that the wind and waves would obey His command. We, the Body of Christ, have this same authority.

INTRODUCTION
THERE IS A WAR

THERE IS A SPIRITUAL BATTLE going on, and, though you may not be able to see it with the natural eye, you need to be aware of it. There is an enemy working against you, and it may surprise some of you to discover that it's not your husband or your wife; it's not your co-worker or your boss; it's not that pesky neighbor or the bill collector – it's Satan. He is the *real* adversary.

Many Christians have adopted a humanistic view of life. That means that when they look at their situations and circumstances, the things that happen to and around them on a daily basis, they see only the natural realm. They view life purely on a surface level, assuming that most everything they encounter is physical or natural. The truth is that there is a battle raging every single day in the spiritual realm. Your real enemy, Satan, is waging an all-out war trying to steal the hearts of people from God. After all, the devil's "job description" is to "steal, kill and destroy," and he is very good at what he does.

Yet, the sons of God are made manifest in the earth today to destroy the power of the wicked one. To be saved by the power of God is to be brought from the realm of the ordinary into the extraordinary, from the natural into the divine. The divine plan is that you increase until you receive the measureless fullness of God.[1]

Even so, some Christians want to bury their heads in the sand. They think that if they simply ignore the devil, he will go away and stop bothering them. Nothing could be further from the truth! Other Christians deny that a spiritual battle even exists. They think that if they don't enter into the battle, then the battle isn't there. Nothing could be further from the truth! Just because you can't see it in the natural doesn't mean that the war isn't raging. It just means that you are going to lose.

However, once you recognize that the war is real, you can learn how to fight back. Paul says that we are fighting the good fight of faith, and here is the best part: we are fighting a battle in which the enemy has already been defeated. You heard it right! Jesus defeated Satan over two thousand years ago with His death, burial, and resurrection! Now, our Champion Jesus is seated at the right hand of God in victory, and we are seated there with Him in the courts of Heaven.

Very few believers who are saved by God's grace have a correct understanding of how great their authority is over the devil and all of his works. In this book, we are going to explore this battleground and our authority together. You will discover that Satan is indeed defeated, and you will also find tools to help you in your fight of faith against him. You will see who you are in Christ and where you are positioned spiritually. The more sure you are of how great your God is and who He has fashioned you to be as a new creation in Christ, the more confident you are to walk in the authority He has given you. It is a real joy when the believer recognizes the inheritance he has in Christ Jesus.

So who is this enemy who dares to wage war against God's anointed, chosen ones?

CHAPTER ONE

KNOW THY ENEMY

"So that Satan will not outsmart us. For we
are familiar with his evil schemes."
(2 Corinthians 2:11)

T
HE POLICE PROCEDURAL, or police crime drama, is one of the most popular television formats today. People love a good detective show, with the traditional who-done-it formula looping the viewer in for some forty-five to fifty minutes. Most of these story-lines feature a no-nonsense detective who always gets to the bottom of the case, using various means, one of which may be *profiling*. He assesses and analyzes a suspect's behavior and characteristics to determine if that person is capable of a crime. Some of the most celebrated

crime procedural shows on television today make good use of the concept of *profiling* in their story-lines.

In his book, *The Art of War*, Chinese general and military strategist Sun Tzu penned a chapter entitled "Strategic Attack." From this, he made a well-known statement: "Know thy enemy; know thy self." Even a worldly army general understood this biblical principle, and, by it, won many battles. So why is it so important that we know our enemy and how he operates? It is **"so that Satan will not outsmart us. For we are familiar with his evil schemes"** (2 Corinthians 2:11 NLT). We have to remember who the real enemy is: **"For we wrestle not against flesh and blood, but against principalities, against powers, against the rulers of the darkness of this world, against spiritual wickedness in high [places]"** (Ephesians 6:12).

Here are some facts about your adversary, the devil, and his demons. Take some time, and study what the Word of God says regarding him so that you can "Know thy enemy":

- Demons are called *devils* (Mark 16:17), *familiar spirits* (Leviticus 20:6), *unclean spirits* (Mark 1:27), *evil spirits* (Luke 7:21), and *seducing spirits.* (1 Timothy 4:1)
- Demons are evil. (Judges 9:23; 1 Samuel 18:10)
- Demons are made subject to Christ and His body of believers by the Word of God (Matthew 8:16), the Blood of Jesus (Revelation 12:11), the Name of Jesus (Luke 10:17), the Holy Spirit (Matthew 12:28), and by the angels, the hosts of Heaven. (Revelation 20:1-3)

- Thousands of demons can enter into and take possession of one man at the same time. (Mark 5:9)
- Devils must be discerned (1 Corinthians 12:10), tested (1 John 4:1), resisted (James 4:7; 1 Peter 5:8-9), and rejected. (Ephesians 6:10-18)
- The rightful place for demons is in the abyss. (Luke 8:31; Revelation 20:1-3)
- Devils have separate personalities. (Luke 8:26-33)
- Devils are disembodied spirits. (Matthew 12:43-45)
- Devils are Satan's emissaries. (Matthew 12:26-29)
- Devils are numerous and seek to enter in/control both man and beast. (Matthew 12:43-45; Mark 5:1-18; Luke 8:32-33)
- Demon possession and demonic influence are different. (Matthew 4:23-24, 16:21-23)
- Demons know their fate to be one of torment. (Matthew 8:29)
- Demons know those who have power over them. (Acts 19:13-17)
- Demons believe there is one God and fear Him. (James 2:19)
- Demons make war on the saints. (Ephesians 6:10-18)
- Demons influence men to sin. (1 Timothy 4:1)
- Satan is a liar and the father of lies. (John 8:44)
- Demons are liars. (1 Kings 22:21-22)
- Devils are unclean. (Luke 4:36; Revelation 16:13-14)

We are in a war, and we need to understand who the real opponent is. Many of the laws that govern the earth today came into being when Adam sinned, and the curse came upon the earth. But because people don't understand this, they go through life blaming God for sickness, strife, poverty, natural disaster, and every other evil work. Even insurance policies call storms, earthquakes, floods, etc., "acts of God." They are not acts of God! They are acts of the devil!

Besides understanding who the devil is, "Know thy enemy" means recognizing his strategies and devices. Some of the works of the enemy are:

- possession of both humans and animals (Mark 5:1-18)
- causing dumbness and deafness (Mark 9:25)
- blindness (Matthew 12:22)
- grievous vexation (Matthew 15:22)
- lunacy and mania (Matthew 4:24)
- uncleanness (Luke 4:36)
- self-harm (Mark 5:5)
- suicide (Matthew 17:15)
- epilepsy (Mark 9:17-22)
- convulsions (Mark 9:20)
- lusts (John 8:44)
- stealing, killing, destroying (John 10:10)
- counterfeit worship (Psalm 106:37-38)
- error (1 Timothy 4:1)
- sickness and disease (Matthew 10:1)
- oppression (Acts 10:38)

- torment (Matthew 4:24)
- deception (1 Timothy 4:1-2)
- lying (1 Kings 22:21-22)
- enchantments and witchcraft (1 Samuel 28; 2 Chronicles 33:6)
- heresies and false doctrines (1 Timothy 4:1)
- wickedness (Luke 11:26)
- fear (2 Timothy 1:7)
- worldliness (1 Corinthians 2:12)
- bondage (Romans 8:15)
- discord (James 3:16)
- violence (Matthew 28:8)
- betrayals (John 13:2)
- sin (1 John 3:9)
- persecution (Revelation 2:10)
- jealousy (1 Samuel 18:6-11)
- false prophecy (1 Kings 22:21-24)

Just look at the works of the Son of God in comparison. Did Jesus ever bring on a storm, cause sickness, curse with lack and poverty, or produce death? No! Instead, He calmed the storm, healed the sick, generously provided for the needs of the people, and raised the dead. We must discern who the real adversary is and not allow him to deceive us. There used to be a saying in the Church: "God is *good*, and the devil is evil." God *is* good, and His mercy endures forever (Psalm 100:5). God is also love (1 John 4:16), and **"love worketh no ill to his neighbor"** (Romans

13:10). Therefore God worketh no ill towards you. You have to settle this fundamental truth in your heart.

Furthermore, to "Know thy enemy" means that spirits must be tried, discerned, and judged. The Bible addresses this subject many times and tells us how to assess them, even admonishing and encouraging us to **"believe not every spirit, but try the spirits whether they are of God"** (1 John 4:1a). In this Scripture, John instructs us to ask them whether Jesus Christ has come in the flesh and find out what they say about Him.

The Holy Spirit has been given to us to assure us that we are the children of God. He will help us realize and really comprehend that He who is in us is greater than he who is in the world (1 John 4:4). Concurrently, the unction we have from the Holy One and His Anointing causes us to know all things and to know "who is who" by the Spirit of God (1 John 2:20-27). He is the Helper who will aid us in discerning spirits, whether or not they are from God.

Reverend Kenneth E. Hagin pointed out that on several occasions, as he was "in the Spirit" going down the prayer line praying for people, he would ask individuals to repeat after him, "Jesus Christ has come in the flesh." Some, in turn, would reply, "Jesus Christ has *not* come in the flesh." Brother Hagin knew right then and there they had to cast an evil spirit out first in order to minister further to that person.

2 Corinthians 11 talks about deceivers, false apostles, and false prophets, who are of their father, the devil. Satan comes as an angel of light but dispels no darkness at all. Christ Jesus

our Lord came to **"destroy all the works of the devil"** (1John 3:8). The devil's number one work is to corrupt our minds from the simplicity that is in Christ. 2 Corinthians 11:3 points out that we overcome and prevent great bondage, captivity, and condemnation by our simple obedience to God. We take our authority, not questioning our Father's simple commands, but questioning and getting to the source of the one trying to deceive us by putting us into captivity through his lying appeals.

To help us discern the works of the enemy, we have the great and mighty Holy Spirit of Truth. He will expose the lies of the devil spoken through false prophets and deceivers and keep us from bondage. I tell people often, "'Believe God's prophets and you will prosper' (2 Chronicles 20:20), but believe false prophets, and you will go broke!" 1 Corinthians 12:3 also declares that anyone speaking by the Spirit of God will never call Jesus accursed. Everyone speaking by the Spirit of God will say Jesus is Lord. Revelation 19:10 tells us, **"The testimony of Jesus is the spirit of prophecy."**

There is another reason why we must "Know thy enemy," and that is to avoid what the military calls "friendly fire." Too many times, in the Body of Christ, we are suffering from wounds that are self-inflicted. In other words, instead of dealing with the real enemy, Satan and his cohorts, we are busy fighting flesh and blood, fighting each other. Psalm 133 says that the anointing is poured out because there is unity among the brethren. No unity - no anointing. No anointing - no freedom from bondage, for it is the anointing that destroys the yoke (Isaiah 10:27).

As we mentioned previously, metaphorically sticking our head in the sand will not make the devil disappear; neither will pretending that he doesn't exist. Peter warns us in 1 Peter 5:8, **"Be sober, be vigilant; because your adversary the devil, as a roaring lion, walketh about, seeking whom he may devour."** We need to be on guard, thoroughly versed in the Word, because demons are illegal holders of authority who will take advantage of the ignorant believer. It is essential to know what the Bible says about our adversary's character, strategies, and tactics, thus preparing us for when the attack comes.

However, this is only one side of the coin; there is another crucial truth we must become intimately acquainted with, and that is to "Know thy self."

CHAPTER TWO

KNOW THYSELF

ONE OF THE MOST IMPORTANT foundational truths for the born-again believer is knowing who you are in Christ. It is much easier to walk in authority when you boldly declare: "I know **'whose I am and whom I serve'**" (Acts 27:23). Consider this: a police officer will confidently carry out his duties because he knows that he ultimately has the backing of the municipal government. For instance, when he stands at a busy intersection and blows his whistle to direct traffic, he expects people to obey his directions. Why is this? He knows he is an officer of the law operating under the authority of the chief of police who, in turn, serves at the pleasure of the mayor. He knows "whose he is" (a police officer working for the municipal government) and "whom he serves" (the police department for whom he works).

Now in light of this, consider our role as the Church. We often hear the term "Body of Christ," but what does that mean? The answer is in 1 Corinthians 12:27, which says, **"Now ye are the body of Christ, and members in particular."** You, the born-again believer, are the Body of Christ, and we know that every "body" needs a "head." Ephesians 1:22-23 says God, **"hath put all things under his feet, and gave him to be the head over all things to the church, which is his body, the fullness of him that filleth all in all."** So we see from these Scriptures that Jesus is the Head of the Church (Colossians 1:18), and we are His Body. If the Head, Jesus Christ, has authority, then the Body, His Church, has this same authority. The head does not operate separately from the body and vice versa. If all things are **"put under his feet,"** then all things are put under our feet as well because we are His Body, His feet on this earth.

When we grasp this simple truth, we boldly declare, **"Herein is our love made perfect, that we may have boldness in the day of judgment: because as he is, so are we in this world"** (1 John 4:17). We should interpret Jesus' life and ministry in the light of this Scripture. How did Jesus walk the earth? Was He intimidated by the devil? No! 1 John 3:8 states, **"For this purpose the Son of God was manifested, that he might destroy the works of the devil."** If Jesus walked around destroying the works of the devil, and "as He is, so are we in this world," what should we as His Body be doing right now? Right! Destroying the works of the devil! Romans 8:19 says, **"For the earnest expectation of the creation eagerly waits for the revealing of the sons of God"** (NKJV). The King James Version says, **"the manifestation of the sons of God."** All of creation is waiting for *you* to take your place in the Body of Christ. It is waiting for *you, as His Body,* to be manifest in the earth as God's arrow against the enemy. **"Like arrows in the hand of a warrior, so are the children of one's youth"** (Psalm 127:4 NKJV).

In Exodus 15:3, Moses and the Israelites recognized that **"The LORD is a warrior; the LORD is his name"** (NIV). And in 1 John 3:1, we read, **"Behold, what manner of love the Father hath bestowed upon us, that we should be called the sons of God."** We see that the Lord is the Warrior, and we are His children. We are His arrows, sent to carry out His authority, declaring His Word throughout the earth. If we look a little further in 1 John 3:2, we read, **"Beloved, now are we the sons of God, and it doth not yet appear what we shall be: but we know that, when he shall appear, we shall be like him; for we shall see him as he is."** If God has destined us to be like Jesus, if that is the destination of our character, our whole being, then we will not be ashamed to take authority over the enemies of our God.

"I have been crucified with Christ; it is no longer I who live, but Christ lives in me; and the life which I now live in the flesh I live by faith in the Son of God, who loved me and gave Himself for me" (Galatians 2:20 NKJV). When we fully comprehend who we are in Christ and the love that the Father has for us, we will be **"filled to the measure of all the fullness of God"** (Ephesians 3:19), until all our enemies acknowledge 1 John 4:4: **"Ye are of God, little children, and have overcome them: because greater is he that is in you, than he that is in the world."** This is God's divine plan and purpose for His family. This is who we are in Christ.

Remember 2 Corinthians 5:21, **"For he hath made him to be sin for us, who knew no sin; that we might be made the righteousness of God in him."** Religion will tell you that you are a "sinner saved by grace." Not true! Jesus *became* your sin. You *were* a sinner, but when you asked Jesus into your heart, you became a **"new creature"** in Christ: **"Old things are passed away; behold, all things are become new"** (2 Corinthians 5:17). You are *not* that sinner anymore. According to 2 Corinthians 5:21, you are the righteousness of God in Christ.

Hebrews 10:14 also declares, **"For by one offering he hath perfected for ever them that are sanctified."** So Jesus Christ has *perfected* you for all time. Even though your spirit man, the real you, will grow and develop, you are still perfect. Even though your mind, the way you think and process things, has to be renewed daily, you are perfect. Even though your body must be brought in line with God's Word, *you are perfect* in His sight. Don't let your heart condemn you! God says that He certainly doesn't. **"There is therefore now no condemnation to them which are in Christ Jesus, who walk not after the flesh, but after the Spirit"** (Romans 8:1). You can walk in freedom today, knowing that your heavenly Father loves you and that all of

Heaven is backing you as you take your authority on this earth against the devil who is the adversary of all mankind.

Let's put ourselves in remembrance of who we are in Christ as born-again believers by meditating on the following Scriptures. Declare these over yourself every day until your thinking comes in line with what God's Word says about you.

I am:

. . . born again by the Word of God. (1 Peter 1:23)

. . . a new creation in Christ. (2 Corinthians 5:17)

. . . a child of God. (Romans 8:16; Galatians 3:26)

. . . greatly loved by God. (Romans 1:7; Ephesians 2:4; Colossians 3:12)

. . . the righteousness of God in Christ. (2 Corinthians 5:21)

. . . a partaker of His divine nature. (2 Peter 1:4)

. . . God's workmanship, created in Christ for good works. (Ephesians 2:10)

. . . alive in Christ with all my sins forgiven. (Colossians 2:13)

. . . redeemed from the curse of the law and blessed with the Blessing of Abraham and the Spirit of Promise. (Galatians 3:13; Galatians 3:9)

. . . free from the law of sin and death. (Romans 8:2)

. . . raised with Christ and seated in heavenly places. (Ephesians 2:6; Colossians 2:12)

. . . Christ's ambassador. (2 Corinthians 5:20)

. . . the Body of Christ. (1 Corinthians 12:27)

. . . united with Christ. (Ephesians 2:6)

. . . created in the image of God. (Genesis 1:27)

. . . conformed to the image of Jesus. (Romans 8:29)

. . . His prized possession. (James 1:18 NLT)

. . . loved, chosen, holy, and without fault in His eyes. (Ephesians 1:4)

. . . a chosen generation, a royal priesthood, a holy nation, His very own possession. (1 Peter 2:9)

. . . a kingdom of priests for God. (Revelation 1:6)

It's vital to get the Word of God into our hearts concerning our redemption and who we are in Christ. Take the time to look these Scriptures up, and write them out on your own. Study them, and get them into your heart by meditating on them day and night until your mind is completely renewed.

Every born-again believer in Christ, filled with the Holy Ghost evidenced by praying and worshiping God in unknown tongues, has the power to:

- **Overcome all sin and bad habits.** (Matthew 1:21; Romans 6:14, 8:2; Ephesians 1:7, 2:1-9; 1 John 1:7-9, 2:29)

- **Cast out demons.** (Mark 16:17; John 14:12; Acts 8:7, 16:18)
- **Be endued with power from on high to be His witnesses.** (Luke 24:49; Acts 1:8)
- **Be immune from poisons** (Mark 16:18; Acts 28:2-6)
- **Control wild beasts.** (Psalm 91:3, 13; Mark 1:13; Luke 10:19)
- **Heal everyone prayed for.** (Matthew 4:24, 8:16-17, 9:35, 12:15, 14:36, 21:14; Luke 4:40)
- **Raise the dead.** (Matthew 10:7-8; Hebrews 11:11-12, 35))
- **Bind and loose anything.** (Matthew 18:18)
- **Destroy the works of Satan.** (Acts 10:38; John 17:18; 1 John 3:8, 4:17)
- **Fully preach the Gospel of Christ through mighty signs and wonders by the power of the Spirit of God.** (1 Corinthians 2:4; Romans 15:19)
- **Receive everything prayed for according to the Word of God.** (Matthew 6:4-6, 18, 7:7-11, 20-21; Mark 11:22-24; 2 Corinthians 1:20)
- **Control the elements.** (Matthew 21:18-22; Mark 4:35-41; John 14:12)
- **Execute judgment.** (Acts 5:1-11, 13:6-12; 1 Corinthians 5:12-13)
- **Get abundant provision for life.** (Matthew 6:25-33; Luke 11:2-3)
- **Exercise authority over all the power of the devil.** (Luke 10:19)

- **Have complete knowledge of the truth beyond all doubt.** (John 7:16-17, 8:31-32, 14:16-17, 26, 16:7-15; Colossians 2:7)
- **Pray and worship God.** (Ephesians 5:16-20; Colossians 3:16-17)
- **Speak with unknown tongues, having rivers of living water flow from his belly.** (John 7:37-39; Acts 2:1-11, 38-39, 5:32; Romans 8:26-27; 1 Corinthians 14:18)
- **Have freedom from darkness and experience complete light.** (John 8:12; Acts 26:18; 2 Corinthians 3:18; Ephesians 4:17-21; 1 John 1:7)
- **Have power to do the works of Christ and even greater works than He did.** (Mark 16:15-20; John 14:12-15; 1 Corinthians 12:4-11; 2 Corinthians 10:4-5)
- **Have healing and sound health.** (Romans 8:11; 3 John 2; 1 Peter 2:24)
- **Have the gifts of the Spirit.** (1 Corinthians 1:5, 7, 12:4-11, 31; Romans 12:6-8; 1 Peter 4:11)
- **Impart the gifts of the Spirit to others.** (Romans 1:11; 1 Timothy 4:14; 2 Timothy 1:6)
- **Have the fruit of the Spirit.** (Galatians 5:22-24)

So we see that God has already done His part. Sin is not an issue with God because Jesus took all the sin of mankind upon Himself. **"The next day John seeth Jesus coming unto him, and saith, Behold the Lamb of God, which taketh away the sin of the world"** (John 1:29). The sins of the entire world - past, present, and future - have already been forgiven. Now *you*, as a Christian, can stand in the presence of God without a sense of guilt or inferiority. Now *you* have the right to use the authority that Jesus bought and paid for with His precious Blood.

Chapter Three

God-Inside Minded

I N 1 JOHN 4:4, JOHN DECLARES: **"Ye are of God, little children, and have overcome them: because greater is he that is in you, than he that is in the world."** The Body of Christ needs this revelation now more than ever - we must be "God-inside minded." Understanding that the Creator of the universe, the Almighty God, El Shaddai, is the One abiding in you, causing you to pray bold prayers.

You are a part of the Body of Christ, a member of His Body, and Jesus is the Head. Therefore, whatever the Head has, the Body has as well. For instance, Luke 4:18-19 says, **"The Spirit of the Lord [is] upon me, because he hath anointed me to preach the gospel to the poor; he hath sent me to heal the brokenhearted, to preach deliverance to the captives, and**

recovering of sight to the blind, to set at liberty them that are bruised, to preach the acceptable year of the Lord." If the Spirit of the Lord is upon Jesus, then the Spirit of the Lord is upon me. I can do the same works Jesus did when he walked the earth and even greater works, thereby bringing glory to the Father (John 14:12).

In Acts 3, Peter and John commanded the lame man who begged outside the temple gate called Beautiful to rise up and walk. We know by reading verse sixteen that they were acutely aware that it was God's power and the Name of Jesus that healed the man: **"By faith in the name of Jesus, this man whom you see and know was made strong. It is Jesus' name and the faith that comes through him that has completely healed him, as you can all see."** But at the same time, we see that this healing power was under Peter's authority, and it was up to him to use it. Faith in the Name brought about the miracle, but Peter had to act on the authority given to him.

Also, notice that Peter didn't ask God to heal this man. He believed Jesus had already done His part and had placed His healing power inside of Peter. Now Peter and John had to choose to release that power by faith in the Name of Jesus. Being "God-inside minded," they grabbed that beggar by the hand and saw the miraculous happen right then and there!

The prophet Isaiah had a revelation of this, saying, **"So shall they fear the name of the LORD from the west, and his glory from the rising of the sun. When the enemy shall come in like a flood, the Spirit of the LORD shall lift up a standard**

against him" (Isaiah 59:19). So we see that the Holy Spirit, who lives inside of every believer, is working on our behalf, pushing back the works of darkness. We also see that the Father, whom you belong to, is **"more powerful than anyone else. No one can snatch them from the Father's hand"** (John 10:29). No demon in hell, no devil on earth, no principality, no power can separate you from the love of the Father because He is the greater one who lives in you (1 John 4:4)!

Take some time, and meditate on what Paul wrote in Romans 8:38-39 because it will change the way you view yourself and your relationship with God. **"For I am persuaded, that neither death, nor life, nor angels, nor principalities, nor powers, nor things present, nor things to come, nor height, nor depth, nor any other creature, shall be able to separate us from the love of God, which is in Christ Jesus our Lord."** If I were to take Romans 8:37-39 and paraphrase it using the *King James Version*, the *Amplified Bible*, the *New International Version*, and the *New Living Translation*, I would get something like this:

> "In all these situations, we are more than conquerors and gain an overwhelming victory through Him who loved us [so much that He died for us].
>
> "For I am persuaded [and continue to be convinced — beyond any doubt] that neither death, nor life, nor angels, nor principalities

(demons) - not even the powers of hell can separate us from God's love.

"Neither things present nor the future, nor any powers [in the sky above or in the earth below], nor height, nor depth, nor any other created thing (or anything else in all creation), will be able to separate us from the [unlimited] love of God, which is [revealed] in Christ Jesus our Lord."

How great is the love of the Father toward us! When we are "God-inside minded," seeing ourselves the way He sees us, and knowing how much He loves us, we walk confidently in that love on this earth, executing His Word every single day.

Always remember that Christ Jesus has given you His authority over the enemy. Daily remind yourself of Luke 10:19, keeping it before your eyes: **"Behold, I give unto you power to tread on serpents and scorpions, and over all the power of the enemy: and nothing shall by any means hurt you."** You are fighting from a place of victory, not from a place of "trying to get the victory." You are not the sick *trying* to get healed. You *are* healed by His stripes, and the devil is trying to make you sick!

Be determined to develop your faith in this area. Have faith in God, knowing Who is dwelling on the inside of you. Get your "speaker" hooked up to your "believer." Then you will be able to talk back to the mountain in front of you. You will tell it what to do, and it will be cast into the sea where it will be swallowed up forever, never to be seen again.

Chapter Four

The Holiest Plan
for the Release
of His Power

I N JOHN 14:1-4 JESUS SAID, **"Let not your heart be troubled: ye believe in God, believe also in me. In my Father's house are many mansions: if [it were] not [so], I would have told you. I go to prepare a place for you. And if I go and prepare a place for you, I will come again, and receive you unto myself; that where I am, [there] ye may be also. And whither I go ye know, and the way ye know."**

We have heard this Scripture read at many funerals, but, in actuality, it is not a funeral passage! When Jesus said, **"I go to prepare a place for you,"** He was talking about the place of *authority,* not a house of brick or stone. His plan was to go ahead of us to make ready that dwelling place of dominion for His Body, the Church. When you read John 14:3, **"I go to prepare a place for you,"** think of a turtle sitting on the fence post. How in the world did he get up there? We all know that the turtle did not end up there by himself. He can't climb the post. He can't fly. Someone *lifted* him and *placed* him there. In the same way, the Body of Christ cannot climb to the place of authority. Jesus had to lift us and place us there. However, Jesus could not raise us to that position of authority until He had first gone there Himself.

Consider what Jesus said to Mary in John 20:16-17 when she caught Him just as He was on His way to present His Blood to cleanse the heavenly Mercy Seat: **"Jesus saith unto her, Mary. She turned herself, and saith unto him, Rabboni; which is to say, Master. Jesus saith unto her, Touch me not; for I am not yet ascended to my Father: but go to my brethren, and say unto them, I ascend unto my Father, and your Father; and [to] my God, and your God."** The Mercy Seat in the Old Testament was "the Holiest," and only the high priest could enter there once a year to present an offering for the sins of the people. This was a type of the Mercy Seat in Heaven. Jesus had to ascend there first to present the offering of His Blood before He could lift Mary there, before He could raise His Body to be seated in the heavenly places.

Why did Jesus have to ascend to Heaven ahead of His Church? We see the answer to this in what happened in the Garden of Eden at the very beginning. Adam committed high treason against his

Creator, selling-out his God-given authority over all creation to the devil. That mercy seat became tainted by Adam's sin. From that point, God the Father looked at man through glasses of judgment, and by the law, He judged. BUT the Good News is that when Jesus presented His Blood, the tainting of the Mercy Seat was removed. Because of His sacrifice, the Father now looks at us through His *mercy*. The war between God and man is over.

This is also why Jesus told Nicodemus in John 3:16-17, **"For God so loved the world, that he gave his only begotten Son, that whosoever believeth in him should not perish, but have everlasting life. For God sent not his Son into the world to condemn the world; but that the world through him might be saved."** He then told His disciples to **"Go ye into all the world, and preach the gospel to every creature"** (Mark 16:15). His Gospel can be likened to a "gos-pill." It is Good News.

- Good News to the sinner: your sins are forgiven, and you are free from the bondage of iniquity.
- Good News to the sick: the price was paid, and by Jesus stripes, you are healed
- Good News to the poor: Jesus Christ became poor so that we through His poverty would be made rich

The Good News is that Jesus restored us to the place of authority that God had bestowed on Adam in the Garden.

Just as the turtle had to be lifted up and placed on the fencepost, so Jesus had to lift up and place His Body into its position of authority. We read in Ephesians 2:4-6, **"But God, who is rich in mercy, for his great love wherewith he loved us, even when we were dead in sins, hath quickened us together with Christ, (by grace ye are saved;) and hath raised [us] up together, and made [us] sit together in heavenly [places] in Christ Jesus."**

This sitting together in the heavenly holiest place is a position of authority whereby the believer will rule and reign in life. Furthermore, according to Ephesians 1: 19-23, **"And what [is] the exceeding greatness of his power to us-ward who believe, according to the working of his mighty power, which he wrought in Christ, when he raised him from the dead, and set [him] at his own right hand in the heavenly [places], far above all principality, and power, and might, and dominion, and every name that is named, not only in this world, but also in that which is to come: and hath put all [things] under his feet, and gave him [to be] the head over all [things] to the church, which is his body, the fullness of him that filleth all in all."**

Now when you read this passage, it might seem that there are three seats in the holiest place: one for God the Father, one for Christ Jesus, and one for us the believer as we take our place in Him. However, there are actually only *two* seats: our seat with Christ in the heavenly places where we are seated "**far above all principality, and power, and might, and dominion, and every name that is named**," and, by consequence of that heavenly seat, our physical position here on this earth whereby we exercise that authority to rule and reign over all the works of the enemy.

Jesus told His disciples that in His Father's house are many *mansions*. When we look up the word "mansions" in the Greek, we get a better picture of what Jesus meant regarding the seat of authority He has placed us upon. The word "monē[1]" implies a temporary or permanent abiding. It means "a staying, abiding, dwelling or abode." This definition is very compelling because, in Psalm 91, we read, **"He that dwelleth in the secret place of the most High shall abide under the shadow of the Almighty."** This abiding comes by saying of the LORD that **"[He is] my refuge and my fortress: my God; in him will I trust."** That "secret place" is *here*, on earth, where we take our seat in Christ. He is seated next to God the Father, and we are seated with Him in the heavenly places, far above all of the devil's nonsense.

Just as a natural house has many rooms, I believe that the rooms in this place or seat we have in Christ in the Holiest represents a place of abiding in prayer, communion, and fellowship with God our Father as we are seated *in* Christ. We are exhorted to be **"instant in prayer"** (Colossians 4:2 DRA) by the Apostle Paul, who also asserted that the believers are to pray **"always with all prayer and supplication in the Spirit, and watching thereunto with all perseverance and supplication for all saints; and for me, that utterance may be given unto me, that I may open my mouth boldly, to make known the mystery of the gospel . . . that therein I may speak boldly, as**

I ought to speak" (Ephesians 6:18-20). By abiding in Him, we position ourselves in that place of authority whereby we exercise the **"power to tread on serpents and scorpions, and over all the power of the enemy: and nothing shall by any means hurt you"** (Luke 10:19).

Chapter Five

Power in the Name

I
F YOU ARE BORN AGAIN, you have the right and privilege to use the Name of Jesus when you pray. Praying in the Name of Jesus gets God's attention immediately. Why is that? Philippians 2:9-11 tells us the reason: **"Wherefore God also hath highly exalted him, and given him a name which is above every name: that at the name of Jesus every knee should bow, of things in heaven, and things in earth, and things under the earth; and that every tongue should confess that Jesus Christ is Lord, to the glory of God the Father."** In His Name, we have authority to **"tread on serpents and scorpions, and over all the power of the enemy"** (Luke 10:19).

When you call upon someone's name, you are placing a demand on who they are and the authority they possess, whether they are a policeman, the company CEO, or even a parent. The power-backing the Name of Jesus is the power of Almighty God Himself! Mark 16:17-18 shows us that the mighty Name of Jesus – the Name that is above every other name, is the mercury in our thermostat, the flame in our furnace, controlling the atmosphere in which we live. In this passage of Scripture, Jesus, immediately after commissioning His followers for all time to preach the Gospel everywhere throughout the earth, describes the signs that will follow those that believe in this Good News. In other words, if you are a believer, these signs will follow you! Receive that!

So let's take a look at what Jesus says will follow His believers. He declares that *in His Name* they will:

. . . cast out devils

When we read the word "cast," we may think of throwing something, as in casting a line for fishing. But the Greek word for "cast," which is "ekballo[1]," actually means to drive something out with a show of force, violently. In Luke 19:27, Jesus told His disciples that He saw Satan fall like lightning out of Heaven. I believe this illustrates what "casting the devil out" really means. God the Father cast Lucifer out of Heaven when the devil tried to exalt himself above God, and thus Jesus saw him fall from Heaven as lightning. Lucifer was driven out "with a show of force, violently." Similarly, when we resist the devil, he flees from us in terror; much like turning on the light causes the darkness to flee.

Luke 9:1 says that Jesus gave His disciples power and authority over all devils. We have this same power and authority, and we must act on it because, **"The thief cometh not, but for to steal, and to kill, and to destroy: I am come that they might have life, and that they might have [it] more abundantly"** (John 10:10). Therefore, it is *our* responsibility as the Body of Christ to cast the enemy out. We are commanded to **"Neither give place to the devil"** in any area of our lives (Ephesians 4:27); we are to forbid demonic manifestations in Christ Jesus' Name.

1 Peter 5:8 tells us, **"Be sober, be vigilant; because your adversary the devil walks about like a roaring lion, seeking whom he may devour"** (NKJV), but when we resist the devil, he *will* flee from us in terror just like when he was cast out of Heaven (James 4:7). Note that it says the devil is roaming about *like* a roaring lion. It doesn't say that he *is* one. Jesus didn't just knock Satan's teeth out through His death, burial, and resurrection. He stripped him of all power and authority, and we need to see our enemy as he truly is. Isaiah 14:16 says that one day the nations will look at Satan in astonishment and say, **"Can this be the one who shook the earth and made the kingdoms of the world tremble"** (NLT)? So remember your position in Christ, and use your authority to drive the enemy out.

We must understand that, while Mark 16:17 certainly speaks of casting devils out of human beings, as Jesus displayed throughout His ministry here on the earth, it also means casting devils out of every area of our lives. Rebellion has no place in our kids; poverty and lack have no business in our homes; sickness has no right in our bodies. In Jesus' Name, we cast these things out! Open your mouth and say, "In Jesus' Name, I bind you, devil, and I cast you out! I drive you out of my home, my children, my marriage, my finances, and my body in the Name of Jesus! Go! Leave now!"

- ● ... speak in new tongues

Paul the Apostle, in his letter to the Corinthian church, talks about speaking with the **"tongues of men and of angels"** (1 Corinthians 13:1) – not having learned them, but having been given them by the Holy Spirit, speaking the wisdom of God in a mystery as the Spirit gave him utterance. Jesus said, **"These signs shall follow them that believe"** (Mark 16:17c). Therefore, tongues are a sign **"not to them that believe, but to them that believe not"** (1 Corinthians 14:22). Tongues are the supernatural evidence of the Holy Spirit's indwelling.

Once, I heard Pastor Kenneth Hagin Jr. speak on this verse. He asked, "What sign do you have for unbelievers who come to your church if you take tongues out?" I then said to myself, "I'm going to prove this out!" So every time since, when I share the Gospel with someone who says they are an atheist who doesn't believe in God, I immediately start praying in tongues out loud right in front of them. Everyone almost immediately asks what language I am speaking. I tell them, "It's supernatural. I never learned it, but it comes from the Holy Spirit. The Holy Spirit listens in on what Jesus is praying in Heaven and gives me utterance to pray the same thing. When I pray this way, I come into agreement with Christ Jesus, and God's will is done on the earth as it is in Heaven." Almost every time, the person listening to me pray in my heavenly language will get born again and start speaking in tongues as well!

. . . take up serpents, and if they drink any deadly thing, it shall not hurt them

Did you know that walking in divine protection is a sign? For instance, when we read Psalm 91, we see how God protects those in covenant fellowship with Him. Just as the Israelites were protected from the angel of death by the blood of lambs splattered against the doorposts of their houses, so we as born-again believers walk in divine protection. That blood-covenant protection was a sign to every Egyptian that not one Israelite would be affected by plague or darkness or death (Exodus 9:4; 11:7). Likewise, walking in divine protection is a sign to unbelievers that the God you serve and have a covenant with is a good God.

In the summer of 1987, after my first year at Rhema, my family went to California to a church camp at Pine Valley Retreat. One night, my uncle asked if I would lead the evening devotions around the campfire. Excited at the opportunity, I skipped supper and went out to the ball diamond with my Bible and my notebook. I planned to do a sermon by Billy Sunday called, "Givin' the Devil His Due."

As I was walking back along the path to my cabin, singing and worshiping God, all of a sudden, I froze. On the ground about three feet in front of me was a rattlesnake, all cocked and ready to strike. Now, we don't have rattlesnakes in Edmonton, Alberta, where I'm from, so you can imagine my surprise. I immediately pointed at it and said, "You cannot hurt me. Get out of here right now, in Jesus' Name!"

The snake didn't budge; he just lay there, rattling. Scriptures started going through me like Luke 10:19, Genesis 1:28, Philippians 2:10, and the whole of Psalm 91! I pointed at that snake again and declared, "No deadly thing will harm me! Get out of here! You'll not hurt me!"

It continued rattling.

Then I saw some people walking by, going towards a cabin in the distance. I shouted at them, "Hey! Come, help me!"

They never heard me. They just kept walking and disappeared into the cabin.

Now Scripture started pumping through me like machine gun bullets, and this time I pointed at the snake and commanded it: "Leave NOW!!! IN JESUS' NAME! YOU CANNOT HURT ME!"

That old snake shot off into the woods like a bullet, and I went on my merry way, praising God for His authority.

. . . lay hands on the sick, and see them recover.

In Matthew 10:7-8, Jesus sent His twelve disciples out in pairs to share the Good News. Look at what He commanded them: **"And as ye go, preach, saying, The kingdom of heaven is at hand. Heal the sick, cleanse the lepers, raise the dead, cast out devils: freely ye have received, freely give."** Look very carefully; He didn't say, "Ask Me to heal the sick," He said, "You heal the sick." Many times Christians "circumnavigate" their prayers for healing, meaning that they will pray about it, they will ask God to do it, they will plead with Him to heal the sick, but the truth is this: God has placed His healing power under our authority. It is time for us to become commanders instead of beggars. Isaiah 45:11 says, **"concerning the works of my hands command ye me."** What does this signify? Does it imply that we are mightier and more powerful than God? Certainly not. He is referring to calling into existence the things He has already done. We need to take our authority and command God's power instead of passively asking God to do what He told us to do. Then we will see the miraculous result for which we are praying.

*****

In Jesus' Name, we are to do the works that He did and even greater works (John 14:12). One way that we do the works of Jesus is by using His Name to take dominion over the natural realm of this earth. Let's take, for example, this first-hand account in Matthew 8, where we read about Jesus taking authority over the weather:

"And when he was entered into a ship, his disciples followed him. And, behold, there arose a great tempest in

the sea, insomuch that the ship was covered with the waves: but he was asleep. And his disciples came to [him], and awoke him, saying, Lord, save us: we perish" (vs. 23-25).

Jesus was asleep in the boat expecting His disciples to deal with the weather using *their* faith. When they failed to do so, He taught them a first-hand lesson on authority! He dealt with that storm then and there with three words: **"Peace, be still"** (Mark 4:39a). His disciples were astounded: **"And they feared exceedingly, and said one to another, What manner of man is this, that even the wind and the sea obey him"** (Mark 4:41)? They had the fear of God put into them when they realized that Jesus was not some ordinary rabbi - He had authority!

Mark 11:22-24 declares that when we have faith in God, our "speaker" (our mouths) will be hooked up to our "believer" (our faith), and we will talk back with authority to the mountain in front of us. We will tell it what to do using the Name of Jesus, and it will be cast into the sea where it will be swallowed up forever, never to be seen again. Notice that Jesus tells His disciples in John 14:13-14, **"And whatsoever ye shall ask in my name, that will I do, that the Father may be glorified in the Son. If ye shall ask any thing in my name, I will do [it]."** It is His will that we use His Name on this earth because then the Father is glorified.

I can testify to using the Name of Jesus on numerous occasions in my own life. I grew up on a farm, and if you know anything about farming, you know that the weather plays a significant factor. As a teenager, in the summer of 1982, I was baling hay at my dad's homestead in Warburg, Alberta, Canada, alongside my uncles. As the day progressed, we looked up to see a dark black cloud coming straight for the field we were farming in. I jumped up on top of the tractor seat and spoke to that cloud. Using the authority I have in Christ, I shouted, " In the Name of Jesus, you are *not* dropping a drop of water on this field. I'm taking this crop in dry!"

My uncles told me to take cover in the house at the east end of the field where I was baling, but I stood my ground. Everyone else went into the house, but I kept right on baling hay. The cloud passed over our land and poured rain at the east end of the field where our property's fence line was. Not a drop of rain hit our crop. I just kept bailing hay in the sunshine!

I remember another time, several years later. I was working at the east end of the Whitemud Freeway, where a number of us were just starting to take off two hundred acres of wheat. Clouds were all around us, filling the sky and threatening to put a stop to our work for the day. My dad jumped into the combine with me and said, "We need to pray because it looks like it's going to rain." So we agreed together in Jesus' Name. I prophesied out of my mouth: "It is *not* going to rain on this field. We are going to haul this crop in dry!"

That day it rained all around us in a circle, but it did not touch that field all day. We hauled that crop of wheat in dry. We stood on the Word of God and used our authority in the Name of Jesus. We knew that the devourer could not touch our increase because we pay our tithes and offerings. Malachi 3:11 declares that God will rebuke the devourer for our sakes concerning our crops, investments, and income.

There are many more personal examples I could give about using the Name of Jesus, but know this for sure: **"The name of the LORD [is] a strong tower: the righteous runneth into it, and is safe"** (Psalm 18:10). When you confessed Jesus as Lord and believed in your heart that God raised Him from the dead, God delivered you out of the power of darkness and translated you into the kingdom of His dear Son - the kingdom of light. You are saved. You are God's child and have every right to use the Name of Jesus. You have entered into His Name by receiving God's free gift of salvation. Ephesians 3:15 confirms it: **"Of whom the whole family in heaven and earth is named."** Just as my wife took on the surname of "Sabo" when we got married, and my daughters took on my name when they were born, so you took on the Name of Jesus, and all that it entails, when you made Him Lord of your life.

So now the ball is in your court. Matthew 10:1 reads, **"And when he had called unto [him] his twelve disciples, he gave them power [against] unclean spirits, to cast them out, and to heal all manner of sickness and all manner of disease,"** and Jesus has given us the same power. We are His Church, His Body, called by His Name to take authority over the enemy and cast him out. We are to heal the sick. And we must do it because God has done everything He will ever do about our problems at the cross.

CHAPTER SIX

POWER IN THE BLOOD

"*A*ND THEY OVERCAME HIM by the blood of the Lamb, and by the word of their testimony; and they loved not their lives unto the death" (Revelation 12:11). There is so much hope, so much power in this one Scripture! You are going to overcome! Why could John, the one who penned the book of Revelation, so confidently make this declaration? The reason is John heard Jesus say, **"These things I have spoken unto you, that in me ye might have peace. In the world ye shall have tribulation: but be of good cheer; I have overcome the world"** (John 16:33). John had an epiphany: Jesus has overcome the world, and, therefore, *we* have overcome with Him!

What is it about the Blood of Jesus that makes us more than conquerors? To start with, we know that Mary was **"found with child of the Holy Ghost"** (Matthew 1:18c), so that means that the Blood of Jesus Christ is holy, not being of human origin. And with this Blood, we are *redeemed*, or another word we could use is *purchased*.

For this reason, the Blood of Jesus is of much more value than gold or silver. It is exceedingly precious, more costly, and possessing a much stronger buying power than silver or gold, or any other material object on this earth. Therefore, even the world's economic market cannot be determined by material objects, nor is it stabilized by gold or silver. The world's economy is determined by the number of people who know they are redeemed (bought) with the precious Blood of Jesus Christ - the Lamb without spot or blemish.

Furthermore, *blood* and *life* are synonymous - **"For the life of the flesh is in the blood"** (Leviticus 17:11) - and mankind has been bought with the Blood of Jesus. Although when the spirit of a man leaves his body, the body is dead, we experience resurrection life through the Blood of Jesus. Jesus infuses the spirit of a man through His resurrection power, sustaining the body, soul, and mind of the believer in Christ. The life of Jesus is always being made manifest in our mortal flesh because of His Blood.

The Blood of Jesus is the reason why we can walk in authority every day. Think about this: Lucifer and one-third of the angelic host rebelled against God. For that reason, they were cast out of Heaven to the earth, thereby taking mankind into captivity. Concurrently, through His Blood sacrifice, one-third of the Trinity, Jesus Christ Himself, delivered all mankind from those rebellious spirits cast out of Heaven. **"For if by one man's offence death reigned by one; much more they which receive abundance of grace and of the gift of righteousness shall reign in life by one, Jesus Christ"** (Romans 5:17,19). So we see it is because of the Blood of Jesus that we reign in life.

What else does the Blood of Jesus do?

- It cleanses us from all sin. (1 John 1:7; Revelation 1:5)
- It redeems us. (Hebrews 9:12; 1 Peter 1:18-19; Revelation 5:9)
- It sanctifies us and makes us holy. (Hebrews 13:12)
- It gives us life. (John 6:53)
- It cleanses our conscience from dead works. (Hebrews 9:14 NKJV)
- It brings us near to God. (Ephesians 2:13)
- It gives us boldness to enter into the Holy of Holies. (Hebrews 10:19)

The Blood of Jesus Christ is the only access into the Holiest of Holies, which we, as believers, can enter boldly. The Blood of Jesus is the new and living way, which Christ Jesus has consecrated for us, through the veil, which is Christ's flesh. Now, **"[having] an high priest over the house of God; let us draw near with a true heart in full assurance of faith, having our hearts**

sprinkled from an evil conscience, and our bodies washed with pure water" (Hebrews 10:21-22).

Without the shedding of blood there is no remission of sin (Hebrews 9:22). Jesus shed His precious holy Blood for us all so that we would become part of the family of God and exercise His authority on the earth. No one ever spilled a drop of blood for the sin of the world except Jesus. By doing so, He not only bore away our sin, but all of our sickness, disease, and poverty, so we are made righteous and whole through Him. Just as He told the Pharisees regarding the paralytic on the mat: **"For whether is easier, to say, [Thy] sins be forgiven thee; or to say, Arise, and walk? But that ye may know that the Son of man hath power on earth to forgive sins, (then saith he to the sick of the palsy,) Arise, take up thy bed, and go unto thine house. And he arose, and departed to his house"** (Matthew 9:5-7). Jesus was making a point that the Blood, *His* Blood, which saves your soul, is the same Blood that will make you whole.

So we see that there is so much power in the Blood of Jesus that is available for us believers. Why, then, do we see so many in the Body of Christ sick and wanting, poor and defeated? To answer this question, let's look at Romans 3:24-25. **"Being justified freely by his grace through the redemption that is in Christ Jesus: whom God hath set forth [to be] a propitiation through faith in his blood."** In other words, the power that releases redemption comes through faith in the Blood of Jesus. Faith in His Blood brings the promises of God into reality! By pleading the Blood of Jesus in, on, and all over yourself, others, or situations, you are being like a judge throwing down his gavel and saying, "It is finished. Devil, back off. The Blood of Christ Jesus declares, 'I'm healed. I'm righteous. I'm blessed, and on the victory-side, and Jesus is Lord!'"

But remember, **"Faith cometh by hearing, and hearing by the word of God"** (Romans 10:17). So, just like any other principle in God's Word, you must make the Word of God concerning the Blood of Jesus your final authority. If you don't know what the Word says about the power of the Blood, it will do no good for you to plead the Blood of Jesus. It's the revelation-knowledge about the Blood that you hold in your heart that will cause the words you speak to have power.

Now perhaps you can see why the enemy fights so hard to keep believers from talking about the Blood of Jesus. As the old hymn goes, "There is power, power, wonder-working power in the Blood of the Lamb." Have you ever wondered why churches don't sing about the Blood anymore? It's because the more you make of the Blood of Jesus, the more God will make of you, and the devil doesn't want that! When you study the Blood of Jesus, talk about it, sing about it, faith comes to you. Faith in that Blood rises up on the inside of us until we declare boldly, "No more, Devil! I am redeemed by the Blood of Jesus! I take authority over you in Jesus' Name!"

So how do we apply the Blood of Jesus in our lives - how do we "plead the Blood?" Just as the Israelites had to apply the blood of the sacrificial lamb a certain way, to the doorpost of each house, and that first Passover is a type and shadow of Jesus, our Passover Lamb, we too, as believers, have to apply the Blood of Jesus a certain way. Firstly, one of the most important keys to pleading the Blood of Jesus is being connected to His Body, the Body of Christ. Just like a foot cannot receive blood flow if it is disconnected from the body, you cannot walk in complete authority apart from being connected first to Jesus and then to the local church.

Secondly, you must apply the Blood of Jesus by faith. You must know in your heart that you have the right to use the Blood of Jesus by faith. Speak it over yourself. Paint it on your doorpost of your life by proclaiming it over your family, your body, your finances, etc. Psalm 45:1 declares that your tongue is the pen of a ready writer. Use your "pen" by proclaiming, "I plead the Blood of Jesus over my family, my body, my finances in the Name of Jesus."

The Blood and Body of the Lord Jesus Christ, the Bread of Life, is the doorway into miraculous wonders and the power of God for your life and family. It is God's glorious salvation and provision set before you. You will plead the Blood of Jesus often when you realize that the power of God backs it and brings with it your blessing and provision. It's a legal term that tells the devil to back off - the price was paid. When nothing else seems to work, plead the Blood of Jesus.

There are some excellent reference materials to go through on the Blood of Jesus to feed your faith and starve your doubts to death. Mark and Tina Hankins have many resources, including books, downloads, CDs, and DVDs on the Blood of Jesus. You may also consider reading Wendy Varga's book entitled "Sacred Secret." Faith in God works miracles and imparts the great and mighty Holy Spirit of Promise!

Chapter Seven

More Power Tools

THERE IS MUCH TO BE SAID about each one of these power tools we are about to explore. Although I could write a book about every single one of them, I am going to touch on each one briefly as it pertains to using your authority:

The Prayer of Faith

Perhaps you've heard about the importance of praying in faith, but what does that mean? How do you do it? The prayer of faith is a vital part of your journey as God's child, regardless of where you are at right now spiritually. Part of learning about your authority in Christ is learning about the prayer of faith - what it is and how to do it.

Let's look at what Jesus said to His disciples in Mark 11:22-25. There are some key points here and, if you spend some time with this Scripture, they will unlock your understanding in this area. **"And Jesus answering saith unto them, Have faith in God. For verily I say unto you, that whosoever shall say unto this mountain, Be thou removed, and be thou cast into the sea; and shall not doubt in his heart, but shall believe that those things which he saith shall come to pass; he shall have whatsoever he saith. Therefore I say unto you, what things soever ye desire, when ye pray, believe that ye receive [them], and ye shall have [them]. And when ye stand praying, forgive, if ye have ought against any: that your Father also which is in heaven may forgive you your trespasses."**

The first thing Jesus said in this passage is to "Have faith in God." Correctly translated, this also means, "Have the faith of God," or, "Have God's faith." When you pray, it is essential to do so in faith because **"without faith [it is] impossible to please [him]: for he that cometh to God must believe that he is, and [that] he is a rewarder of them that diligently seek him"** (Hebrews 11:6). If you don't have faith, you won't even bother coming to God in prayer. Faith is the key to having your prayers answered - you can't bring about Spirit-led change in your life or the life of others without it. Faith finds out what God's Word has to say and prays in accordance. The prayer of faith stands on God's Word alone.

Developing a consistent prayer life and living in constant fellowship with the Father through the Holy Spirit is vital. When you pray daily, remember what James 5:16 says: **"The earnest (heartfelt, continued) prayer of a righteous man makes tremendous power available [dynamic in its working]"** (AMPC). Look at the example of the prophet Elijah in 1 Kings. Elijah told King Ahab that it was not going to rain until he said it would, and indeed, there was no rain in the land until Elijah prayed. The Bible called his prayer an "effectual prayer."

The prayer of faith will also cause you to **"Pray without ceasing"** (1 Thessalonians 5:17), until you see the manifestation of God's promise in your life. It means continually declaring and decreeing the same thing. For example, the woman with the issue of blood kept saying to herself, "If I only touch His garment, I shall be restored to health" (Matthew 9:21 AMPC).

Here are four things you must do to practice the prayer of faith and thereby walk in authority:

1. Say it.

In Mark 11:23, Jesus instructs His disciples that they are to **"*say* unto this mountain."** You've got to talk back to your mountain. Life and death are in the power of *your tongue*, not the mountain, not your doctor, not your banker, nor the circumstance that is standing before you. If you knew what was on the other side of your mountain, you would move it into the sea of forgetfulness with your words.

Praying the prayer of faith means speaking and proclaiming what you want. **"Thou shalt also decree a thing, and it shall be established unto thee: and the light shall shine upon thy ways"** (Job 22:28). You've got to talk back to your mountain. Tell it, "You will be no more," and watch it disappear into the sea of forgetfulness. Don't talk the problem, but declare what you are going to have in Jesus' Name. Be an imitator of God, our Father, and of Abraham who, **"believed God, who quickeneth the dead, and calleth those things which be not as though they were"** (Romans 4:17).

At the beginning of creation, when God looked out over the earth and saw darkness covering it, He never said, "Oh, it's sure dark out there." God said, "Light, be," and *light was.* Likewise, Abram had a promise from God for many years, yet it wasn't until the Angel told him, **"Neither shall thy name any more be called Abram, but thy name shall be Abraham; for a father of many nations have I made thee"** (Genesis 17:5), that Abraham actually started to declare who he was. Abraham literally means "Father of Many Nations." When he fought and won a battle, the kings would ask him what his name was, and Abraham would answer, "Father of Many Nations."

"How many kids do you have?" they would ask.

Abraham would say, "I'm the 'Father of Many Nations.'"

His servants would call him, "Father of Many Nations," every time they used his name – Abraham – and all the while, Abraham was being surrounded by words of faith and love – the Truth. It was nine months later that Sarah had "Ha! Ha!" – Isaac, whose name means "Laughter." Laughter and joy will always be born out of your declaration of faith. People who claim Abraham as their father need to *act* like their father – as children of faith!

2. Believe it.

The very foundation of your Christian walk is faith, so it stands to reason that every prayer you pray must be rooted in faith. Romans 12:3 tells us, **"God hath dealt to every man the measure of faith"** the moment they asked Jesus into their heart as Lord and Savior, but faith must be grown, and we do that through hearing the Word of God (Romans 10:17). We believe what we speak the most. Your voice is your "mailbox" in the realm of God.

Consider Abraham, who **"against hope believed in hope, that he might become the father of many nations, according to that which was spoken, so shall thy seed be."** Romans 4:19-21 continues to tell us Abraham considered not his own body and staggered not at the promise of God, but was strong in faith, giving glory to God. Abraham was fully persuaded that what God had promised, He was also able to perform. He consequently received that promise because he believed God was faithful to follow through on His Word.

3. Receive it.

Whether you see an immediate result or not has no bearing on your prayer of faith. Faith believes before it receives the promise; before the five senses perceive the answer. By faith, see yourself healed, see the bill paid, see that cancer removed. Trust God's Word, and know that **"God's way is perfect. All the LORD's promises prove true. He is a shield for all who look to him for protection"** (Psalm 18:30 NLT). By believing that God raised Jesus from the dead, the promises of God are imputed to us as well. They are yours.

4. Act on it.

"In the same way, faith by itself, if it is not accompanied by action, is dead" (James 2:17). We must act on our faith concerning what God's Word says about our situation. How would you conduct yourself if the promise was yours today - if you saw the manifestation of it right now? What would you be doing if you already had it? How would you talk? Faith should always have a corresponding action. Prepare for the promise to be so.

The Spirit of Faith is an attitude. **"We having the same spirit of faith, according as it is written, I believed, and therefore have I spoken; we also believe, and therefore speak"** (2 Corinthians 4:13). What you believe will affect your whole attitude about life. Once faith changes your attitude, your outlook on life will be changed, and so will your actions. Believing is an attitude we have that God is greater, His Word is higher, and that Jesus is mightier than any situation or circumstance. It is the attitude that what is unseen is beyond the limits of what is seen. In other words, when I have faith in God, I believe and therefore speak, and my words will have a corresponding action.

One ingredient of faith is the refusal to quit and give up. The Spirit of faith has an attitude of persistence and patience. The Spirit of faith always causes you to rise to the top. Philippians 4:13 tells us that we can do all things through Christ (the Anointed One and His Anointing) who strengthens us. In other words, with this Spirit of Faith, I can control my attitude, even in the midst of all kinds of adversity, **"being confident of this very thing, that he which hath begun a good work in you will perform [it] until the day of Jesus Christ"** (Philippians 1:6). Press on, knowing that your best days are still ahead. Your best Blessings haven't even happened yet. God is in the middle of every circumstance you're in, and the worst situation you could possibly face is being turned around and worked into something good by your loving Father.

So, refuse to give up. When you incorporate these four areas into your prayer life, you will begin to see yourself walking in greater authority. Winston Churchill said, "If you are going through hell, keep going." The real glory is not in getting knocked down to your knees but in getting back up again and again. Whatever you do, keep moving forward in Christ Jesus' Name. Choose to persevere. Refuse to be defeated. Nothing in the world can take the place of persistence with the Spirit of Faith.

Tongues

"Likewise the Spirit also helps in our weaknesses. For we do not know what we should pray for as we ought, but

the Spirit Himself makes intercession for us with groanings which cannot be uttered. Now He who searches the hearts knows what the mind of the Spirit [is], because He makes intercession for the saints according to [the will of] God" (Romans 8:26-27 NKJV). The word "helps" means to take hold together against our infirmities or weaknesses. What are our infirmities? We don't know how to pray, as we ought. My natural mind only knows so much, but the great and mighty Holy Spirit knows everything. PC Nelson, a great Greek scholar, pointed out that the phrase **"which cannot be uttered"** literally reads "cannot be uttered in our regular speech" in the Greek.

Praying in our heavenly prayer language is a principle power tool concerning our authority. The devil hates it when believers pray in other tongues because it thwarts his plans against our lives. He can't circumnavigate our prayers when we pray in the Spirit. Praying in tongues allows the Holy Spirit to pray through us the same Word of God that Jesus, our Intercessor, is praying over us. Then Romans 8:28 comes into full view: **"And we know that all things work together for good to them that love God, to them who are the called according to [his] purpose."**

"All things" that we've been praying about start working together when we pray in our heavenly prayer language. As we come into agreement with God and His will for our lives, we will experience **"days of heaven on this earth"** (Deuteronomy 11:21). Praying in tongues will cause our circumstances and situations to come in line with God's will for us. How exciting! No wonder the enemy fights this area!

On top of bringing our natural circumstances in line with the will of God, praying in tongues builds us up in our inner man. Jude 1:20 says it this way: **"But ye, beloved, building up yourselves on your most holy faith, praying in the Holy Ghost."** You are supercharging your inner man like a battery charger. It is like pumping up a tire. Once you have the right amount of pressure, then it doesn't matter what bumps come along your path . . . you just keep rolling right along!

Worship, Praise, and Thanksgiving

"And be not drunk with wine, wherein is excess; but be filled with the Spirit; speaking to one another in psalms and hymns and spiritual songs, singing and making melody in your heart to the Lord; giving thanks always for all things unto God and the Father in the name of our Lord Jesus Christ" (Ephesians 5:18-20; Colossians 3:16-17). Our "psalming," hymning, and singing spiritual songs are Spirit-led music that keeps us filled with the Holy Ghost who is the greater One living in us. These songs we sing in the Spirit are full of the Word of God and wisdom. They are born of the Holy Ghost, just like speaking in tongues, thereby keeping Jesus Lord over our lives.

The devil despises a worshipper. He would rather see you experience a *breakdown* instead of having a *breakthrough*. Consequently, believers should make worship a lifestyle, lifting hearts of praise to God the Father, both individually and corporately. There will also be times when we must stand in our authority, declaring His will for our lives through praise as King Jehoshaphat did in 2 Chronicles 20. When the enemy pressured Jehoshaphat, he inquired of the Lord, saying, **"Our God, will you not judge them? For we have no power to face this vast army that is attacking us. We do not know what to do, but our eyes are on you."** God responded with this: **"You will not [need] to fight in this [battle]. Position yourselves, stand still and see the salvation of the LORD, who is with you, O Judah and Jerusalem! Do not fear or be dismayed; tomorrow go out against them, for the LORD [is] with you"** (2 Chronicles 20:17).

At this point, the tool that Jehoshaphat pulled out to use against the enemy was not prayer or confession or fasting - it was *praise.* **"And when he had consulted with the people, he appointed those who should sing to the LORD, and who should praise the beauty of holiness, as they went out before the army and were saying: 'Praise the LORD, For His mercy [endures] forever.' Now when they began to sing and to praise, the LORD set ambushes against the people of Ammon, Moab, and Mount Seir, who had come against Judah; and they were defeated"** (2 Chronicles 20:21-22 NKJV).

It is a powerful truth that through our praise God will **"still the enemy and the avenger"** (Psalm 8:2). Praise is just one of several strategies against the enemy that you will find in the Word of God. When you don't know what to do, praise!

Psalm 149:6 says, "**[Let] the high [praises] of God [be] in their mouth, and a twoedged sword in their hand.**" This praise we offer up is in our beds (**v.5**), praising the Lord in tongues and in our natural language. It's worship as we go about our day praying and proclaiming His promises. It's the Word of Truth as we speak it out of our mouths, that two-edged sword effecting change. Because of this, our worship, praise, and thanksgiving carry a supply of the Spirit that will initiate divine intervention on our behalf.

This is you and I, the believer, singing upon our beds, binding principalities and powers that try to rule over us with our worship and the Word of God. By our praise and worship, Jesus continues to destroy the works of darkness and brings them to naught in our lives. My wife and I and our two girls find that singing in tongues before going to bed each night is very powerful and brings immense peace into our home.

Love Walk

"**For in Jesus Christ neither circumcision availeth any thing, nor uncircumcision; but faith which worketh by love**" (Galatians 5:6). Have you ever tried to pray effectually while you are angry with someone or holding a grudge? It's next to impossible! That's why Jesus told His disciples in Mark 11:25, "**And when ye stand praying, forgive, if ye have ought against any: that your Father also which is in heaven may forgive you your trespasses.**" Your love-walk directly affects your faith-walk.

In fact, after each praise direction in Ephesians 5:19-20 and Colossians 3:16-17, we are instructed to submit to one another in the reverential fear of the Lord. It will be challenging to take your authority over the enemy if you aren't doing it by faith, and faith works by love.

Keeping our love walk sharp should be a priority if we want our faith to work right. It's very tough to pick a fight with someone who refuses to fight back because they have decided to walk in the love of God. One way to sharpen our love-tool is to meditate on 1 Corinthians 13, what is often called the "Love Chapter," and pray Philippians 1:9-12 continuously over yourself and others. Doing so will steer your heart and actions towards walking in love with others.

Besides this, **"There is no fear in love; but perfect love casteth out fear: because fear hath torment. He that feareth is not made perfect in love"** (1 John 4:18). Did you know that the opposite of *faith* is not *doubt*? It's *fear*. When you permit yourself to get off the love walk, you open the door to fear. If you allow it, fear will torment you and cause you to doubt every single promise you've been standing on.

Keep your love walk sharp by being a doer of the Word in this area, serving others, and refusing to be offended. **"Great peace have they which love thy law: and nothing shall offend them"** (Psalm 119:65). Be quick to practice kindness and forgiveness so that you can stand your ground against the adversary and effect a tremendous change in your life. **"And be ye kind one to** another, tenderhearted, forgiving one another, even as God for Christ's sake hath forgiven you" (Ephesians 4:32).

Confession of Our Mouths

King David said in Psalm 45:1 that his **"tongue [is] the pen of a ready writer."** If you think of your life as a book with blank pages, each one ready to be penned with the story of all your days, what would you want it to read? If you think of your life as a big ship, with your tongue being the little rudder that steers it, where would you want your course to be plotted? **"For in many things we offend all. If any man offend not in word, the same [is] a perfect man, [and] able also to bridle the whole body. Behold, we put bits in the horses' mouths, that they may obey us; and we turn about their whole body. Behold also the ships, which though [they be] so great, and [are] driven of fierce winds, yet are they turned about with a very small helm, whithersoever the governor listeth"** (James 3:2-4).

As Christians, we have great authority, power, dominion, and victory, given to us by the Lord Jesus. He won them all through His mighty conquest over death, hell, and the grave! Why? So we could be free to choose our own destiny. The rudder of your ship, your tongue, guides you to the harbor in which you are going. The direction your life takes is in direct correlation with the words that come out of your mouth. English Poet William Ernest Henley penned the words, "I am the master of my fate: I am the captain of my soul," in his poem "Invictus." God's Word, the unsurpassable authority, gives us the key to shaping our destiny in Proverbs 18:21, which tells us that **"life and death are in the power of the tongue."** *You* have control over your own life. *You* have the ability, the authority over your own destiny, to choose which one you want - life or death. *You* are the one who **"will also declare a thing, and it will be established for you"** (Job 22:28 NKJV).

God used words to create and frame the world. He made us in His image to do the same thing with ours. The words we choose to speak, especially when spoken in agreement with the Word of God, are the most powerful tool we have on earth - our address in the Spirit realm. **"For by your words [reflecting your spiritual condition] you will be justified and acquitted of the guilt of sin; and by your words [rejecting Me] you will be condemned and sentenced"** (Matthew 12:37 AMP). When you do things God's way, you will never fail to live in the Blessing. **"So too, faith, if it does not have works [to back it up], is by itself dead (inoperative and ineffective)"** (James 2:17 AMP). Therefore, since I **"have faith in God"** – the God kind of faith, I talk back to the mountains I face and tell them to be gone into the sea of forgetfulness. I believe I receive what I ask for from God my Father, and I receive it (Mark 11:22-24).

As an example, God's animal, the horse, has been man's helper throughout the ages. Horses pull heavy loads and carry various riders, and God gave man a way to cause horses to obey us so they could be useful helpers. There is a place in the horse's mouth where teeth do not grow, where owners put bits in their mouths to lead them wherever they want them to go. The way to guide a horse is through his mouth.

God wants to guide us with the words of our mouths. His Word is like the bit in the horse's mouth. If we speak God's Word, He will help us stay under control. To be a workhorse for Jesus, a good and effective helper, we need to speak scriptures over ourselves and others. We need to obey God's command of walking in love. As a result, every time we speak the Word of God, it is a sword coming out of our mouths. It is a trumpet blown in the enemy's ears, announcing our victory. Jesus gave us the authority, the power to change our lives by the very words we speak, so let that mountain hear you pronounce the Word of God with authority.

Fasting

Fasting does not give us spiritual power and authority. Jesus has already given us all authority in heaven and on earth. (Luke 10:19) When He rose from the dead, Jesus declared, **"All power is given unto me in heaven and in earth. Go ye therefore, and teach all nations, baptizing them in the name of the Father, and of the Son, and of the Holy Ghost"** (Matthew 28:18-19). He also declared, **"These signs shall follow them that believe; In my name shall they cast out devils; they shall speak with new tongues; they shall take up serpents; and if they drink any deadly thing, it shall not hurt them; they shall lay hands on the sick, and they shall recover"**

(Mark 16:17-18). James 4:7 tells us that we are to **"Submit yourselves therefore to God. Resist the devil, and he will flee from you,"** and Ephesians 4:27 says to **"Neither give place to the devil."** We have all power and authority over the devil and his cohorts in Jesus' Name as children of God and joint-heirs together with Christ.

The New Testament does not command us to fast. However, we are directed and encouraged to live a fasted life, so we are not **"brought under the power of any"** (1 Corinthians 6:12). Jesus tells us in Matthew 26:41 that we are to, as good soldiers, watch and pray to avoid temptations, tests, and trials. We are to be ready in season and out of season, ready to preach the Word of God, the Word of faith, which is the Good News of the Lord Jesus Christ, as Paul says in 1 Timothy 4:2. Fasting is one way we can bring our body into subjection to our spirit where healing and the Holy Ghost-quickening come from.

Fasting is a valuable spiritual tool to control our fleshly appetites, so we are not body-ruled, but Spirit-ruled, Spirit-led. We are kings and priests unto God our Father, and therefore rule and reign in life with Christ Jesus. Our fasting, or bringing our flesh under control, allows the Holy Spirit's leading and workings to be made manifest, as we are Spirit-led to break every yoke (Isaiah 58:6-8).

Let's take a look at what the prophet Isaiah says about fasting in Isaiah 58:

"Is it a fast that I have chosen, A day for a man to afflict his soul? [Is it] to bow down his head like a bulrush, And to spread out sackcloth and ashes? Would you call this a fast, And an acceptable day to the LORD" (v.5)? God is not looking at the things you give up for a fast, whether they be food, TV, or even coffee! He is looking at your heart-attitude.

"[Is] this not the fast that I have chosen: To loose the bonds of wickedness, To undo the heavy burdens, To let the oppressed go free, And that you break every yoke" (v.6)? This verse shows us what God wants the outcome of our fasting to be.

"[Is it] not to share your bread with the hungry, And that you bring to your house the poor who are cast out; When you see the naked, that you cover him, And not hide yourself from your own flesh" (v.7)? Fasting is not about doing what we want, but in our fast, reaching out to others.

"Then your light shall break forth like the morning, your healing shall spring forth speedily, and your righteousness shall go before you; the glory of the LORD shall be your rear guard. Then you shall call, and the LORD will answer; you shall cry, and He will say, 'Here I [am].'" I know of a minister whose body was sick and not responding to the Word of God, so he told his body, "I'm going to fast until you receive the Word and divine health flows into you." And that is exactly what happened - he was healed!

Fasting and living a fasted life are valuable tools. When you fast, you are setting yourself up to win. You are giving God room to work in your life, creating space for absolute victory.

Communion

There are two types of communion addressed in the Word of God. The first is the Holy Communion, also referred to as the Lord's Supper (John 6:47-58, 63; 1 Corinthians 11:20-34). Although we partake of the Lord's Supper at church with other believers, we don't have to wait until we go to church to receive Communion (1 Corinthians 11:26). We can receive it anytime and anywhere. Taking the time to put ourselves before God over the Communion table reminds us of what Jesus bought and paid for at the cross.

Taking Communion is the most powerful and significant celebration in which the believer can participate. It is holding up the Blood Covenant we have with God our Father, Jesus Christ our Lord, and the Holy Spirit, and declaring before them, before the angels of God, and before the devil and his cohorts that we are Blood-Blessed by the Blood of Jesus. Communion declares to the devil that the price was paid for your forgiveness, and you are made the righteousness of God in Christ Jesus. Jesus' body was broken and beaten and shredded for you, so now you are the healed, you are the made-strong, just like the man healed in Acts 3. You are the Blood-Blessed with the Blessing of Abraham (Galatians 3:13-14). You are blessed with all spiritual Blessings in heavenly places in Christ Jesus (Ephesians 1:3).

God instituted Communion for the first time in Exodus 12, and the *first* is always a precedent for the rest. The children of Israel partook of the lamb, applying its blood to their doorposts and, before they walked out of the land of their captivity, they were loaded by the Egyptians with silver and gold and whatever else they wanted! As well, the miracles of healing that took place after they applied the blood were so great that **"there was none feeble among His tribes"** (Psalm 105:37 NKJV). We are talking about over five million people - not one sick, not one feeble among them!

Yet now we are living under the New Covenant, with better promises, a better priesthood (Hebrews 8:6), so how much more powerful is Communion for us with God as our Father and Christ Jesus as our Blood Brother and the Holy Spirit of Promise as our surety. You can bank on the heavenly protection and deliverance that the Father has given you through the Blood of Jesus. Gifts of healing and supernatural strength are imparted to your body; witty inventions and revelation knowledge flood your spirit; abundant provision is given unto you, so much so that nations call *you,* "Blessed." This is why Communion is such a significant and glorious celebration for us in Christ. Glory and Hallelujah too!

The second communion is the communion of the saints, being a part of the local church body. When the Body of Christ is in unity, each member doing their part, the anointing of God is poured out on them (Psalm 133). **"But if we walk in the light, as he is in the light, we have fellowship one with another, and the blood of Jesus Christ his Son cleanseth us from all sin"** (1 John 1:7). It is God's will that we have fellowship with other believers. The Church of the Lord Jesus Christ is the most powerful institution in the earth. Individually and corporately, we are the Temple of the Living God. The gates of hell cannot prevail against us when we come together in this holy communion of the saints (Matthew 16:18).

In John 14:12, Jesus made a very emphatic statement: **"Verily, verily, I say unto you, He that believeth on me, the works that I do shall he do also; and greater [works] than these shall he do; because I go unto my Father."** We became the Body of Christ on the earth when Jesus rose from the dead, ascended into Heaven, and took His seat at the right hand next to our Father God. When He left the earth, we became one spirit with Him as Paul tells us in 1 Corinthians 6:17, **"But he that is joined unto the Lord is one spirit."** Now, Jesus doesn't have a bunch of spirits. Christ Jesus has *one* Spirit, and we became one with Him when we declared with our mouths that Jesus Christ is Lord and believed in our hearts that God the Father raised Him from the dead.

Concerning this, we read in Ephesians 1:22-23, **"And hath put all [things] under his feet, and gave him [to be] the head over all [things] to the church, which is his body, the fullness of him that filleth all in all."** God our Father wants us to know His mighty power - the Holy Spirit - Who put all things under Christ Jesus' feet. Technically, as part of His Body, *we are those feet,* and Jesus is the Head over all the Church, which is His Body **"that filleth all in all."** Pastor Arlene Kinzel once said, "The Church is not a religious institution but a living organism filled with the life of God." As His Body, we are His hands and feet here on the earth. In Mark 16:18, Christ stretches out His hands through our hands to heal the sick, break the yoke of bondage and do His works. The devil and all his cohorts and all his nonsense are under our feet.

Now then, we are the Temple of the Living God, individually and corporately. When we come together as the Church, His wisdom is manifest through us to the principalities and powers in the spirit, as we exercise and believe in the authority and power of Jesus' Name. We demand things to be and call them into existence in the Almighty Name of Jesus. In John 14:14, Jesus told us to ask the Father in His Name. This word "ask" in the Greek means "to demand," and is used in the same manner in Acts 3, where Peter and John commanded the lame man to rise up and walk in the Name of Jesus. Just as Jesus enacted authority when he rebuked the fever in Peter's mother-in-law and saw it leave, we as His Body are to use this same authority given to us. That spirit of infirmity had ears to hear and knew Who was telling it to get out, and it left immediately.

Through Jesus' life and ministry on the earth, the Church has been left the blueprint of how to use our authority here. What is remarkable about Christ Jesus' love for us is that God gave all power and authority to Him, and He, in turn, transferred it to us, the Church, which is His Body. Sweatless victory! After all, Jesus did say, **"Take my yoke upon you, and learn of me . . . for my yoke [is] easy, and my burden is light"** (Matthew 11:29-30).

So, as we gather together corporately, plugged into a local body of believers, and attending service weekly, we are being taught and empowered by the administrations of Christ and the gifts of the Holy Ghost. We are being taught how to live and cash in on the Blessing which Christ Jesus our Lord bestowed upon us – how to live in divine health, and how to receive supernatural strength to do the great exploits God has set before us to do. Also, the Church is a place where we are taught where to tithe and sow our seed so that the windows of heaven are opened to us. Then we can receive great favor upon our lives to have more than enough, thus giving into every good work. We are taught at church how rich and full we are, that no good thing does God our Father withhold from us who walk uprightly, living by faith and not by sight.

Binding and Loosing

Jesus gave us the keys to the Kingdom to bind and loose, to lock and unlock. **"And I will give unto thee the keys of the kingdom of heaven: and whatsoever thou shalt bind on earth shall be bound in heaven: and whatsoever thou shalt loose on earth shall be loosed in heaven"** (Matthew 16:19). *You* have the keys to the Kingdom, and the power is in your mouth, your declaration, to execute God's will in this earth. Whatever you declare locked on earth is locked in heaven - not the Heaven where God dwells, but the battle zone, the heaven where Satan's forces are operating - and whatever you declare unlocked on earth is unlocked in heaven.

Jesus has given you all the power and authority that you need to put the devil under your feet. It is up to you now to speak the Word and bind those evil spirits. It is up to you to speak His promises and loose the angelic armies of heaven to work on your behalf. You do this by using the name of Jesus, the Name that is above every other name. At His Name, every knee will bow - in heaven, in earth, and under the earth - and every tongue will proclaim that He is Lord (Philippians 2:9-10).

Don't give any place to the devil. How would we give him place? With our words Proverbs 6:2 says, **"Thou art snared with the words of thy mouth, thou art taken with the words of thy mouth."** Many times we are binding our healing with our mouth and loosing sickness in our lives with careless words like "I am sick to death," or "I am sick and tired . . ." etc. Jesus gave us the power to bind and loose. It's our responsibility to make sure that we are loosing the right thing and not the wrong thing. No doubt talk. Only faith talk.

Submitting to Authority

If you want to walk in authority, you have to be under authority. We see an excellent example of this in Matthew 8. A centurion came to Jesus and pleaded with Him to heal his servant, who was lying at home, paralyzed and tormented by sickness. Without hesitation, Jesus responded, "I will come and heal him."

"The centurion answered and said, 'Lord, I am not worthy that You should come under my roof. But only speak a word, and my servant will be healed. For I also am a man under authority, having soldiers under me. And I say to this [one], "Go," and he goes; and to another, "Come," and he comes; and to my servant, "Do this," and he does [it].' When Jesus heard [it], He marveled, and said to those who followed, 'Assuredly, I say to you, I have not found such great faith, not even in Israel!'" This centurion recognized that Jesus was a man under authority and, consequently, operated in that authority which God gave Him. He realized this same principle in his leadership over a hundred men: if you want to have authority, you must place yourself under authority.

Authority is the direct result of submission and obedience to God and to those He has placed in leadership over us. Our authority is only as powerful as our level of submission to it. James 4:6b declares, **"God resisteth the proud, but giveth grace unto the humble."** Grace and God's favor are synonymous. So ask yourself, "How do I get more favor? How do I humble myself?" We find the answer in the next two verses: **"Submit yourselves therefore to God. Resist the devil, and he will flee from you. Draw nigh to God, and he will draw nigh to you"** (James 4:7-8a).

Our words and actions (works) reveal whom we are submitted to and the destiny we have chosen. Also, the character and nature we are walking in shows to whom we are submitted, listening, and imitating. **"Be imitators of God as dear children"** (Ephesians

5:1 NKJV). Copy Him and follow His example. The real winners are those who are wise enough to develop Godly character and then use the gifts God has given them. The real winners are those who willingly bring themselves under authority.

So to whose authority are we submitting? Well, obviously, as a born-again Christian, the first authority we surrender to is God. **"Submit yourselves therefore to God. Resist the devil, and he will flee from you"** (James 4:7). The key to seeing the backside of the devil as he runs away from you is to submit to God. But the Bible also talks of other people we must submit to:

- Wives must submit to their husbands, as unto the Lord. (Ephesians 5:22)
- We must submit to those in authority over us. (1 Peter 2:13-15)
- We, as employees, must submit to our bosses with great respect, even if we are treated unkindly or unfairly, because it is pleasing to God. (1 Peter 2:18-20)
- We must submit to the governing authorities. (Romans 13:1; Titus 3:1)
- We must submit to our elders. (1 Peter 5:5a)
- We must also be subject to one another. (Ephesians 5:21; 1 Peter 5:5b)

In reality, the entire book of 1 Peter is a reference to our submission to authority, and in the middle of it, we find 1

Peter 2:24: **"Who his own self bare our sins in his own body on the tree, that we, being dead to sins, should live unto righteousness: by whose stripes ye were healed."** It is because Christ submitted to those in authority that He was able to bear our sin, sickness, and poverty, thus gaining us as His brethren. Instead of reviling or fighting back, Jesus submitted to authority, and our redemption was a direct result. In the same way, God has a reward for us as we follow Christ's example.

Consequently, we see that the source of the believer's authority is God. In Psalm 91:13, we read, **"Thou shalt tread upon the lion and adder: the young lion and the dragon shalt thou trample under feet."** Thus, God gave all authority to Jesus in Matthew 28:18. **"Jesus came and told his disciples, 'I have been given all authority in heaven and on earth.'"** Paul also tells us in Philippians 2:9-10, **"Wherefore God also hath highly exalted him, and given him a name which is above every name: that at the name of Jesus every knee should bow, of [things] in heaven, and [things] in earth, and [things] under the earth."**

Jesus, having received all authority from the Father, and the Name that is above every other name, gives the Church this same authority and right to use His Name. **"Behold, I give unto you power to tread on serpents and scorpions, and over all the power of the enemy: and nothing shall by any means hurt you"** (Luke 10:19). As a result, the promise of Genesis 1:26 was restored to all who are born-again into the family of God: **"And**

God said, Let us make man in our image, after our likeness: and let them have dominion over the fish of the sea, and over the fowl of the air, and over the cattle, and over all the earth, and over every creeping thing that creepeth upon the earth." This is the flow of authority in which the Body of Christ must operate.

Chapter Eight

Having Done All, Stand

OURS IS NOT A FIGHT in the natural realm, it is a battle in a spiritual arena, and the weapons of our warfare are not those forged with iron or steel, but they are those of the Spirit. **"For though we walk in the flesh, we do not war according to the flesh. For the weapons of our warfare are not carnal but mighty in God for pulling down strongholds"** (2 Corinthians 10:3-4 NKJV). In Ephesians 6:12, the Apostle Paul counsels us, **"For we wrestle not against flesh and blood, but against principalities, against powers, against the rulers of the darkness of this world, against spiritual wickedness in high places."** We aren't fighting against human beings, those with

"flesh and blood," but we are fighting against a spiritual enemy - one who is defeated! Therefore, our weapons are not "carnal" natural weapons. The weapons we use to take a stand against this spiritual enemy must be spiritual – the armor of God.

Let's take a detailed verse-by-verse look at the armor Paul talks about in Ephesians 6. **"Finally, my brethren, be strong in the Lord, and in the power of his might."** Paul, addressing the Church (his **"brethren"**), commands them to "be strong," not in themselves or even in each other as the Body of Christ, but in the Lord. And in verse 11, he tells them how: **"Put on the whole armour of God, that ye may be able to stand against the wiles of the devil."** We are not standing up against the schemes and plans of man. It is the strategies of the devil, our true adversary, and *his* tactics, lies, and war plans that we are standing against and exposing, just like when Elisha uncovered the plans of the King of Israel's enemy to take his people into captivity (2 Kings 6:8-23).

To be "strong in the Lord" is to be strong in who we are *in Christ* - the Anointed One and His Anointing. Psalm 91 talks about being *in* the Lord - dwelling *in* the secret place of the Most High God, abiding *under* the shadow of the Almighty – and John 15:7 talks about abiding *in* the Word of God and letting His Words abide *in* us. Therefore, being "strong in the Lord" is knowing who we are *in Christ* and not allowing the enemy to tell us otherwise. By constantly affirming who we are in Christ through our words, we gain divine protection making the Lord our refuge and fortress. Ephesians 2:6 tells us that we are seated together *with Christ,* **"far above all principality, and power, and might, and dominion, and every name that is named, not only in this world, but also in that which is to come"** (Ephesians 1:21). We are *in Christ,* and 1 John 4:17 declares, **"as He is, so are we in this world."**

Well, who is Jesus in this world? He is the King of Kings, the Lord of Lords, the Prince of Peace, and we are to be ruling and reigning in life by the One, Christ Jesus (Romans 5:17). Furthermore, we are the righteousness of God *in* Christ Jesus, joint-heirs together *with* Christ, rich and full and reigning in life as kings, owning the gold and the silver with Him . . . the list goes on and on. There are 133-plus scriptures in the New Testament declaring who we are, where we are, what we have *in Christ.* These should be our constant meditation!

Also, we, as believers, are admonished to **"be strong in the Lord and in the power of His might"** (Ephesians 6:10) which is to be full of the Holy Spirit. The "might" of God the Father and Jesus our Lord is the Great and Mighty Holy Spirit of promise, who raised Christ Jesus from the dead and seated Him in the heavenlies at God's right hand. In doing so, the Holy Spirit also raised us up with Christ Jesus - the greatest expression of God's power ever revealed! Death, hell, and the grave could not stop the Holy Spirit from bringing Christ Jesus back to life. To be **"strong in the Lord and in the power of His might"** is to be full of the Holy Spirit, His power working in us. Stephen is a good example. Acts 6:3, 5, 8 declared that Stephen was a man full of faith, wisdom, the Holy Ghost, and power. The Apostle

Paul made **"the Gentiles obedient, by word and deed, through mighty signs and wonders, by the power of the Spirit of God"** (Romans 15:18-19).

To be strong in the Lord and in the power of His might means that we should be doing lots of meditating on who we are in Christ, as well as **"speaking to [ourselves] in psalms and hymns and spiritual songs, singing and making melody in [our hearts] to the Lord"** (Ephesians 5:19), which will keep our joy and peace gauges on full. We should also be praying in tongues a lot, walking by faith and not by sight, and laying hold of the promises of God. These are the things that make us strong in the Lord.

In verse 12, Paul further clarifies whom we are fighting against: **"For we wrestle not against flesh and blood, but against principalities, against powers, against the rulers of the darkness of this world, against spiritual wickedness in high places."** This is the actual warfare that we are waging. Sometimes, we get so caught up in this natural world that we think our battleground is here. We must remind ourselves that it is with the enemy's unseen forces that we contend in the faith. Here is where the movie industry needs to correct itself. Unlike what we might see depicted in a typical Hollywood show, we cannot execute the defeat of dethroned and defeated spiritual beings with natural fleshly weapons. We cannot exercise our authority using guns and knives and swords made of steel. So how do we stand against Satan, the father of lies, who comes to steal, kill, and destroy (John 10:10)? After all, he is, at present, the god of this world and is behind all manner of sickness and disease, poverty and lack, misfortune, and iniquity.

The answer lies in 1 John 5:4. It is our *faith* in God the Father, the Lord Jesus Christ, and the Great and Mighty Holy Spirit that is the victory that overcomes the world. Therefore, we cannot look and listen to anything contrary to our Champion Lover. Christ has defeated Satan and all of his cohorts once and forever. Now it is the Church who must pick up the sword of the Spirit and declare, "It is written! Christ Jesus has spoiled, plundered, defeated, stripped, and made a show openly of the enemy's defeat throughout the chasms of Hades! Death and hell could not contain Him any longer - He has been quickened by the Holy Spirit and raised from the dead!"

Remember that the **"weapons of our warfare are not carnal, but mighty through God to the pulling down of strongholds"** (2 Corinthians 10:4). That is, they are not weapons we can discern with our five senses. They cannot be felt, seen, tasted, etc. They are spiritual weapons that include the armor of God. Paul tells us, **"Wherefore take unto you the whole armour of God, that ye may be able to withstand in the evil day, and having done all, to stand"** (Ephesians 6:13). *Having done all, stand.* Having done everything we know how to do in the natural, we use the armor to stand against the enemy's strategies.

Since a good soldier intimately acquaints himself with his weapons, let's take a close look at ours:

. . . Stand therefore, having your loins girt about with truth (v. 14a)

The belt of truth is a clear understanding of God's Word. In reality, it holds all the rest of the armor in place and anchors our soul. By abiding in the truth of His Word, we have a successful prayer life. It is the filter whereby we judge all matters. However, in order to *know* the truth, we must read our Bibles *on purpose*, allowing His words to abide in us as we abide in them (John 15:7). The truth of His Word is the bedrock, the solid foundation of our faith because the Word is Jesus Himself (John 1:1).

I'm sure you've heard this phrase many times: "The truth will set you free." Tossed around by sinners and saints alike, this sentence has often been misquoted and taken entirely out of context. Let's look at what it really says in John 8:31-32. **"Then said Jesus to those Jews which believed on him, If ye continue in my word, [then] are ye my disciples indeed; and ye shall know the truth, and the truth shall make you free."** Notice that it is the Word of God that we *continue* in that will make us free, not some ambiguous truth floating around in the atmosphere. If we want to know the truth and have the freedom it affords, we will have to make an effort to abide in the Word of God.

Not only must we cultivate a habit of daily Bible reading, but we must also spend time with the Holy Spirit in fellowship and prayer. In doing these two things regularly, we will come to know the voice of the Spirit of God, thereby allowing Him to "guide us into all truth" (John 16:13) When we do this, we will **"Let [our] roots grow down into him, and let [our] lives be built on him. Then [our] faith will grow strong in the truth [we] were taught, and [we] will overflow with thankfulness"** (Colossians 2:7 NLT). Time spent in God's Word and with the Holy Spirit will establish you in the truth.

> **. . . and having on the breastplate of righteousness** (v.14b)

As I mentioned earlier, it is hard to use our authority while floundering in our identity. If my little girls didn't recognize me as their loving father, they wouldn't be able to approach me with confidence. If my wife, Jamie, weren't completely confident in using my name as her husband, she would not act in my stead. They have a position with me in the same way that I have a position with my heavenly Father, seated next to Him in the heavenlies, far above all principalities and powers. I have been given the Name of Jesus so I can ask God my Father for anything He promised me and thus lay hold of it on this earth (Ephesians 1:19-23, 2:6, John 14:13). I recognize that I am a child of God Who is backing me and is for me as I stand against the devil and his nonsense. I know my position in Him.

How we see ourselves is vital when using our authority. Recognizing that you are not just a "sinner saved by grace," but that you are a child of Almighty God gives you boldness to enter the throne room of God. It gives you confidence when confronting the enemy. We are made the righteousness of God in Christ (2 Corinthians 5:21). Therefore we believe what is right until it is made right. If we comprehend Whose we are and Whom we serve and that we are in right standing with Him, we will know that He is on our side. After all, **"If God *be* for us, who can *be* against us"** (Romans 8:31 NKJV)? Nothing can stand in our way.

> **... And your feet shod with the preparation of the gospel of peace** (v. 15)

This peace, which comes from the Anointed One and His Anointing, is the rule or umpire continually in our hearts, directing and governing our lives and thoughts, actions and words. **"And let the peace (soul harmony which comes) from Christ rule (act as umpire continually) in your hearts [deciding and settling with finality all questions that arise in your minds, in that peaceful state] to which as [members of Christ's] one body you were also called [to live]. And be thankful (appreciative), [giving praise to God always]."** (Colossians 3:15 AMPC).

Isaiah tells us we are led forth in *peace* and joy (Isaiah 55:12). Paul talks about the Kingdom of God being righteousness, *peace,* and joy in the Holy Ghost (Romans 4:17). With our feet **"shod with the preparation of the gospel of peace,"** we are making ourselves ready to walk in peace with everyone we meet. Through His Word, we study how to bring peace to every situation.

Through that peace, we look for every opportunity to share the Gospel about Christ Jesus our Savior.

We, the Body of Christ, are called to be peacemakers on this earth our entire life, and all that we are should point others to the way of salvation. We put on the Gospel shoes of peace, laying hands on the sick, casting out devils and stopping all oppression in the name of Jesus everywhere we go. We must **"preach the word; be instant in season, out of season; reprove, rebuke, exhort with all longsuffering and doctrine"** (2 Timothy 4:2). Being "instant" means to be ready, whether the circumstances are favorable or not, always trusting that the Holy Spirit will **"teach you at that time what you should say"** (Luke 12:12 NIV). Your life is the sweet-smelling fragrance of Christ on this earth, and through you, God wants to **"spread the knowledge of Christ everywhere, like a sweet perfume"** (2 Corinthians 2:14 NLT).

> **. . . Above all, taking the shield of faith, wherewith ye shall be able to quench all the fiery darts of the wicked (v. 16)**

Notice that verse 16 says that the believer must *"above all"* take the shield of faith, by which he will be able to *"quench all"* the fiery darts of the wicked. In 1 John 5:4, John tells us, **"For whatsoever is born of God overcometh the world: and this is the victory that overcometh the world, [even] our faith."** We also read in Psalm 5:12, **"For thou, LORD, wilt bless the righteous; with favour wilt thou compass him as [with] a** shield." *Above all,* we are to take up this shield of faith. Our faith in God is like the story we read in 1 Samuel 17 of David taking on Goliath while reiterating to King Saul his previous victories over the bear and the lion. When Saul insisted that David wear the king's armor into battle, David refused. He knew all he needed was faith in his covenant with God.

Entering into the battle, David was insulted by Goliath, who said, "Am I a dog that you come at me with sticks?" David's faith response was, **"Thou comest to me with a sword, and with a spear, and with a shield: but I come to thee in the name of the LORD of hosts, the God of the armies of Israel, whom thou hast defied. This day will the LORD deliver thee into mine hand; and I will smite thee, and take thine head from thee; and I will give the carcases of the host of the Philistines this day unto the fowls of the air, and to the wild beasts of the earth; that all the earth may know that there is a God in Israel. And all this assembly shall know that the LORD saveth not with sword and spear: for the battle [is] the LORD'S, and he will give you into our hands" (1 Samuel 17:45-47).** By faith, David boldly declared his covenant with God, proclaiming that he would conquer Goliath, who didn't have one. Through David's courage and confidence, by raising his "shield of faith," the army of Israel triumphed that day over the Philistines.

Equally, when we stand on our covenant with God brought about through the Blood of Jesus, we are raising our shield of faith. It will quench, extinguish, and silence all the fiery darts of the devil, yes, and even whomever he is using in the natural to shoot them. For example, during a time of intense persecution against her people, the favor of God surrounded Queen Esther like a shield. In that favor, she boldly stood before the king, thereby silencing Haman the enemy and his sons forever. Likewise, this same shield of faith and favor surrounds us, activated by our praise and thanksgiving. We hold fast our confession of faith, trusting our Father to act on our behalf, thereby guaranteeing His promises are ours through the Blood of Jesus.

Furthermore, this shield of faith is to be taken *"above all else."* We must always be on guard, extinguishing every fiery dart the devil throws at us so we can stay in faith in our everyday life. We quench those fiery darts by our faith in God's Word. Thinking faith thoughts and talking faith talk keeps the Holy Ghost generator, our power supply, working on our behalf to produce what we say we believe. The shield of faith activates us to talk back to every mountain we're facing and watch them move into the sea of forgetfulness. Faith thoughts and faith talk prevent the devil from having any place in us. Staying in the arena of faith - the promises of God - enables us to stand against the devil and put him on the run!

. . . And take the helmet of salvation (v. 17a)

Consider what part the helmet played in a soldier's life during the days of Paul the Apostle. Made almost entirely of metal, its most evident value was to protect that soldier against blows to the head. Spiritually speaking, when you put on the helmet of salvation, you remind yourself that you have the mind of Christ. You are no longer conformed to this world. You are transformed by the renewing of your mind (Romans 12:2).

1 Thessalonians 5:8-9 reminds those of us **"who are of the day,"** (born again) to **"be sober, putting on the breastplate of faith and love; and for an helmet, the hope of salvation. For God hath not appointed us to wrath, but to obtain salvation by our Lord Jesus Christ."** We are not to be carnally-minded, which is death, but spiritually-minded, which is life and peace. Consequently, you are kept in perfect peace when your mind is stayed on the Word, Jesus Christ.

Spiritually speaking, the helmet of salvation protects your mind from the blows of the enemy against your thought life. Most of the attacks that come against your mind are rooted in the spirit of fear. Did you know that as a child of the Most High God, you do not have the spirit of bondage again to fear, but the Spirit of adoption by which you cry, "Abba, Father?" It's true! Don't allow the enemy to bully you with the spirit of fear. Straighten that helmet and stand fast in your salvation, knowing that you are born again and no longer subject to the schemes and plans of the wicked one.

"Wherefore gird up the loins of your mind, be sober, and hope to the end for the grace that is to be brought unto you at the revelation of Jesus Christ" (1Peter 1:13). The "loins of your mind" is the procreative ability and imagination of the Holy Spirit. Just like God our Father, we, His children, have this creative ability, and our thoughts need to be activated and directed by the Word of God to such an extent that we look past what *is* and consider what *shall be*. The mind of the Anointed One and His Anointing declares the end from the beginning (Isaiah 46:10).

Furthermore, the helmet of salvation has the peace of God mounting guard over your mind and your heart in Christ (Philippians 4:7). The helmet of salvation is your declaration and awareness of the Lordship of Christ Jesus. He is our Lord and governs our thinking process, enabling us to have His mind, His wisdom, and discernment on every situation and circumstance. We have not the spirit of fear, but we have self-discipline, sobriety, sound mind, and sound judgment (2 Timothy 1:7).

Also, having on the helmet of salvation means that our thoughts are only victorious, like God's thoughts, and we have a victorious mentality. Defeat is not in our vocabulary or thought life. We are more than conquerors through Christ who loves us (Romans 8:37); therefore, a "sound mind" includes a thankful and worshipful mind as well. It is a mind that continually causes our words to bubble over into praises to the Father and Christ Jesus, making us pleasant to be around, being kind and gracious to others.

This helmet of salvation means repeatedly looking to the Spirit of wisdom and revelation to reveal to us our position in Christ (Ephesians 1:17-22). Having on the helmet of salvation is being on the "mind-renewal" program, which Paul talks about in Romans 12:1-2. It is checking in with the Holy Ghost in your spirit, consistently making decisions based on the Word of God and the Holy Spirit's leading. It is following the love of God that has been shed abroad in your heart by the Holy Ghost (Romans 5:5). It is having your mind renewed to know and understand your rights and privileges in Christ because knowing who you are in Him is included in the helmet of salvation. Your mind, the enemy's chief battleground, is protected by the helmet of salvation.

Consequently, "How important is it to put on this helmet of salvation?" you may ask. Well, let me ask you a question in return: "How valuable is your head?" You are a joint heir together with Christ Jesus, Possessor of Heaven and earth, owning all the gold and silver and the cattle on a thousand hills. That helmet is protecting and keeping your mind stayed on Him so that you remain in perfect peace. Then your faith will grow exceedingly, and you will bear much fruit for the Kingdom of God.

. . . and the sword of the Spirit, which is the Word of God (v. 17b)

The sword of the Spirit is the only weapon or offensive piece of armor that we wield. The Word of God is Jesus Christ Himself. In Him, we live and move and have our being, so when we put on Christ Jesus, we stand before our enemy, saying, "It is written." When we speak the Word of God, the enemy is not seeing or hearing us, but the One who defeated and stripped him of his power over us. The Lord is backing us up and putting our enemies to flight when we use the sword of the Spirit. His Word is Christ Jesus – His Name, His Blood, His Word, His deeds, His power, and His Spirit.

You may have accumulated thousands of Bible verses in your heart. You may have a spiritual library inside your spirit man full of shelves piled up with Bible truths and principles. You may have cabinets packed with promises from the Word of God. And you should! But only by following the Holy Spirit's leadership will you be able to reach up with the hand of faith and get the precise truth you need every time. The Holy Spirit will help you to pray both in tongues and in your natural language, accessing the power of God in your life to equip you with wisdom for every circumstance (1 Corinthians 2:7) and the power to overcome.

Jesus said that the words He speaks are Spirit and life (John 6:63). Therefore, the sword of the Spirit is the sword of the Holy Ghost. It is the anointing. It is life. God's Word is anointed, and the Holy Spirit is bringing forth from our spirit that same Word of God. It produces the same wisdom of God, righteousness, redemption, and sanctification that Jesus was made unto us, and now we are made in Christ unto the world as His Body. Faith in His Word is the only weapon with which we defeat the devil every time. It is not by might, nor by power, but by the Spirit of God (Zechariah 4:6). The Holy Spirit is watching over the Word of God to perform it (Jeremiah 1:12).

When you keep the high praises of God in your mouth and a two-edged sword in your hand (Psalm 146:6), you are blowing a trumpet in the ears of Satan, proclaiming what the Word of

God says. When the priests blew the trumpets in Leviticus, it was symbolic of making a decree, announcing their freedom for the enemy to hear. Be diligent in getting the Word deep into your spirit man, store it up, and, like jars of preserves, fill your shelves full of the promises of God. Then when you need that Word, when you need to draw your sword, you will have something to take out of your sheath! You will blow that trumpet of freedom loud and clear for the devil to hear!

By declaring, "It is written," we are bringing to naught the lies and destroying the works of Satan. We are bringing into manifestation the wonderful works of Christ. Talking back to our mountains and holding up the promises of God before our Father and saying, "They are mine," is wielding the sword of the Spirit. Isaiah tells us, **"the yoke shall be destroyed because of the anointing"** (Isaiah 10:27)**,** and God's Word is anointed, so it is the sword of the anointing that breaks Satan's bondage. Take God's holy written Word, and go after any yoke of bondage you are facing, and free yourself and others – with the sword of the anointing! The Holy Spirit and the angels of God go into action when you pick up the sword of the Holy Spirit – the Word of God. So declare and hold up the Word of truth, bringing life and liberty, producing health and prosperity, effecting righteousness, peace, and joy.

. . . Praying always with all prayer and supplication in the Spirit (v. 18a)

Everyone who meets you should be fully convinced that you are filled with the might of God in the Spirit, **"filled with all the fulness of God"** (Ephesians 3:19). Paul tells us in Ephesians 5:18, **"Do not get drunk with wine, for that is wickedness (corruption, stupidity), but be filled with the [Holy] Spirit and constantly guided by Him"** (AMP). Being intoxicated with alcohol is behavior that shows you are absorbed with pleasure, money, and drunkenness, which will eventually end in death. On the other hand, being filled with the Holy Spirit leads to life abundantly, eternally long, and resurrection life. I don't want anything other than being full of the Spirit, and fuller and fuller, until I am overflowing like a great big vat.

By being created anew, born-again, God wants to flow through you with His measureless power of divine utterance and grace until your whole body is a flame of fire. God is not looking for your monuments after being filled with the Holy Spirit in the past. He is looking for you to be a continuous movement in the earth, a movement that knows the glorious truth and breadth of God's almighty power. He wants you to be the salt and light of the earth, clothed in the entire armor of God.

For this reason, take the armor of God by faith, and don't get out of it. The baptism of the Holy Ghost is one to be lost in, where you only know the desire of God at all times. The baptism of the Holy Ghost should be an ever-increasing endowment of power to do mightier works, an ever-increasing enlargement of grace and favor. God intends each person in Pentecost to be a live wire - not a monument, but a movement. Oh, Father God, grant us a real look into Your glorious liberty, which You have designed for the children of God who are delivered from this present world - separated, sanctified, and made suitable for Your use, whom You have intended to be filled with all Your fullness.

*****

Having your armor on, knowing Jesus' victory over Satan and your position in that triumph, there is only one posture of warfare to take against the enemy. Four times in Ephesians 6:11, 13-14, we are told to "stand." We are told to **"put on the whole armour of God, that ye may be able to STAND against the wiles of the devil . . . WITHSTAND in the evil day . . . having done all, to STAND . . . STAND therefore."** We are not commanded to attack but rather to "stand." The believer's position in the good fight of faith is the stand *of* faith, resting on the promises of God. Our stand against the devil is with the Word of God. Our wrestling is not to defeat the devil, for Christ Jesus, our Champion, has already done it for us back at Calvary. Our wrestling is to stand unmoved, unshaken on the Word of God, **"holding forth the word of life"** (Philippians 2:16), and we stand on that Word by resting in His promises by faith.

Again, notice that the reason why we put on the whole armor is to *stand against.* The NIV says that we put on the *full* armor so that we can take our stand against the devil's schemes. Believers have a responsibility to do their own standing! A knight would never run to battle with only a helmet and no sword or shield;

in the same way, we are commanded to put on the entire armor, every single piece, leaving nothing out. And why? So that we can *take our stand* against the devil's schemes. The Amplified Bible says it this way: **"Stand therefore [hold your ground]."**

To hold your ground means to refuse to move backward, especially when you are being attacked. It means to stand up for one's rights, to resist an attack, to refuse to do what someone else wants. It is based on the literal meaning of "stand your ground," which is to stand and fight. It means to defend the ground on which you stand rather than run and give up territory to the enemy as he approaches. It is to remain resolute in the face of opposition. As 1 Corinthians 15:58 says, **"Therefore, my beloved brethren, be ye stedfast, unmoveable, always abounding in the work of the Lord, forasmuch as ye know that your labour is not in vain in the Lord."**

This "standing against" the enemy is something each one of us as believers must do. Jesus, in the garden, told His disciples to watch and pray so that they would not enter into temptation, tests, or trials. So it *is* possible to avoid them. In John 16:33, He told His disciples that, in this world, they would have tribulation. Yet, He also told them to be of good cheer because He had already overcome the world, including the god of this world, Satan. That is why our "stand" is to rest in His promises, clothed in His armor, knowing that Jesus has already won the battle, and the enemy has already been defeated. It is each our responsibility now to do our own standing on the Word of God against the wiles, tricks, war plans, and strategies of the devil himself.

I recall Lester Sumrall's book, "Bitten by Devils," in which he recounts the story of a lady who was bitten continually by an evil spirit. She was delivered only to have that unclean spirit return right after Brother Sumrall cast it out. Rev. Sumrall asked the demon why he was back, at which point the demon responded that, although Brother Sumrall cast him out, the lady wanted him to be there.

Rev. Sumrall cast that evil spirit out again and taught this lady about the authority she had in Christ and how to plead the Blood of Jesus against it. After Brother Sumrall left, that evil spirit came back, but this time the lady resisted it with such authority that afterward, there was found in her clenched fists hair that was of no human origin when placed under a microscope. Nevertheless, the woman was free forever, never again to be tormented by that spirit. She had learned to take her stand against the enemy by using the authority Christ had given her. She had learned to stand with her armor on and resist the enemy. The result was complete and total victory!

Chapter Nine

Bulldog Faith

"*C*AST NOT AWAY THEREFORE your confidence, which hath great recompense of reward. For ye have need of patience, that, after ye have done the will of God, ye might receive the promise" (Hebrews 10:35-36). There is something to be said for the person that won't quit. There is power in persistence. Have you ever played tug-of-war with a dog? Now *they* understand the power of persistence! They won't give up that rope, no matter how hard you pull. That dog knows that if he pulls long enough and doesn't give up, you will eventually let go of the rope. Bulldogs are even more resistant by nature. Their breed and the way they are built is to bite down and not let go.

We need to practice that same tenacity with the Word of God. No matter the pressure or trial, we refuse to let go of that promise until we see the manifestation of it. Rev. Kenneth E. Hagin used to say, "If you are willing to stand forever, you will not need to stand for long." Hebrews 10:38-39 says, **"Now the just shall live by faith: but if [any man] draw back, my soul shall have no pleasure in him. But we are not of them who draw back unto perdition; but of them that believe to the saving of the soul."** We are not of that group who quits on the Word of God. We believe right until the end, right until we see the desired result of our prayers. After all, it is our bulldog faith that will overcome the world (1 John 5:4).

Hebrews 6:12 gives us a fundamental key to answered prayer, one that is often overlooked: **"That you do not become sluggish, but imitate those who through faith and patience inherit the promises"** (NKJV). Faith is not sluggish and lazy; faith is persistent and active. Faith is not passive and undecided; faith is aggressive and determined. But faith has a twin that will help in between the time when the prayer leaves your lips and when you have the manifestation of it in the natural realm. That twin is called "patience." Patience undergirds our faith and gives it the endurance to persevere until the answer comes. Patience is having a confident expectation in God's promises. James 1:3 says, **"Knowing [this], that the trying of your faith worketh patience."** When your faith is tried, it will produce patience, and you must **"let patience have [her] perfect work, that ye may be perfect and entire, wanting nothing"** (James 1:4). When you stand in patience, you will be blessed with every good thing, having every need met according to God's riches in glory by Christ Jesus (Philippians 4:19).

The word "patience" in verse 4 is the Greek word "hypomonē," meaning "cheerful or hopeful endurance."[1] If you think of a long-distance runner, how do they find the strength to run a ten-mile course? They have built up their endurance level starting with one mile, then two, then three, all the way to ten. Similarly, we build up our endurance to the enemy's pressure and our circumstances when we allow patience to work in us. Patience is a confident anticipated expectation that what we believe God said in His Word will most certainly come to pass in our lives. It is a powerful force that will help us hold onto the promise and not let it go.

Bulldog faith is bold and is not afraid to take a stand on the Word against the enemy. Why do you think God told the prophet, Isaiah, **"concerning the work of my hands command ye me"** (Isaiah 45:11)? It is because God wants us to stand our ground on His Word. He is so confident in His promises for us that He is not afraid to back His Word. So we can speak His Word with bulldog faith in complete confidence, nothing wavering.

In all of this, just remember that the devil is persistent. If you think he's going to quit the first time you use your authority, you are wrong. He won't quit the first time with you the same way he didn't quit the first time with Jesus in the wilderness. That devil tempted Jesus to question the very Word God gave Him only four verses before: **"And lo a voice from heaven, saying, This is my beloved Son, in whom I am well pleased"** (Matthew 3:17). The devil came in Matthew 4:3, and what's the first thing he says to Jesus? **"And when the tempter came to him, he said, If thou be the Son of God, command that these stones be made bread."** *If* you are the Son of God.

The enemy will always try to cause you to doubt your identity in Christ and the Word of God so he can steal it from you. But what did Jesus do? He responded with, **"It is written."** You would think that if the Son of God said, **"It is written,"** that devil would flee, running for his life with his tail tucked between his legs. But no, the devil came at Him not once but twice more, three times total, challenging the Word of God given to Jesus.

You better know the devil won't quit on you the first time. He may not even quit on you the second time. But I can guarantee that he is going to let go if you determine that *you* will not quit. He may bombard your mind and with all kinds of excuses why you're not going to receive from God this time. The enemy will attack your mind with thoughts of, "It didn't work this time. You won't get the breakthrough this time. It worked before but not this time." *Don't let go of that promise.* Use your bulldog faith and undergird it with patience. Stand on the Word of God, declaring boldly, "It. Is. Written."

CHAPTER TEN

THE FINAL AUTHORITY

THERE IS AN AUTHORITY that you must determine to submit to if you want to walk in complete and total victory every day - the Word of God. His Word must be the final say in every circumstance and situation. As Kenneth Copeland says, "Put God's Word first place, and make it final authority!"

"I am the Lord, I change not" (Malachi 3:6). Things in this world system are constantly changing, evolving from one day to the next. The world is speeding up faster than ever - technology from the fifties to the eighties has doubled every five years and increased exponentially, to where today it is doubling every five months! Society has been evolving all around us since the induction of the personal computer in the seventies and even more so with the Internet's launch in the nineties. With all this technology and increased knowledge comes change, but there is one thing that remains constant in all the craziness - the Word of God. You can depend on what God says. After all, His Word is:

- perfect. (Psalm 18:30)
- reliable. (Isaiah 40:8)
- never changing. (1 Peter 1:24-25)
- never going to return void. (Isaiah 55:11)
- infallible. (Joshua 21:45)
- Holy Ghost-inspired. (2 Peter 1:20-21)
- never going to disappear. (Luke 21:33)
- growing mightily and prevailing. (Acts 19:20)
- perfect, converting the soul, and sure, making wise the simple. (Psalm 19:7)
- settled in heaven, standing firm and unchangeable. (Psalm 119:89 AMP)
- flawless. (Psalm 12:6 NIV)
- effectually working in those who believe. (1 Thessalonians 2:13)
- healing people, delivering them from destruction. (Psalm 107:20)
- given by inspiration of God. (2 Timothy 3:16)
- profitable for doctrine, reproof, and instruction in righteousness. (2 Timothy 3:16)
- dependable. (2 Samuel 22:31 NLT)

- the principle thing. (Proverbs 4:7)
- able to save your soul. (James 1:21)
- life and health. (Proverbs 4:22)

So we see that if you are a believer, you have something that you can depend on, something that will never change - the Word of God!

If you determine to make what God says in His Word final authority in every matter, you will experience victory in every area. Making the Bible the final authority means believing what God says instead of what others say. It means believing what He says instead of what the devil says. It means believing what He says instead of what your circumstances say. Let the Word of God settle every issue in your life.

Don't allow your circumstances to dictate to you; dictate to your circumstances what the Word of God says. Psalm 103:20 says, **"Bless the LORD, ye his angels, that excel in strength, that do his commandments, hearkening unto the voice of his word."** Those angels stand in the presence of the Almighty and they will never cower or back down. They will only hearken to the Word of God, so put your angels to work by only talking "faith talk." Be cautious of what you say. Determine in your heart to make God's promises the final say in your life. Make up your mind: "Today I choose to walk by faith and not by sight. God's Word says it, and that settles it. My circumstances must line up to what He says."

God does not have a double standard. He doesn't say one thing and will another. So if you are wondering what God's will is concerning your situation, you better open your Bible and find out! Don't let that devil steal your lunch because, **"My people are destroyed for lack of knowledge."** That verse goes on to say, **"Because thou hast rejected knowledge, I will also reject thee, that thou shalt be no priest to me: seeing thou hast forgotten the law of thy God, I will also forget thy children"** (Hosea 4:6). Educate yourself on what the Scriptures say. After all, it isn't the truth that will set you free, but rather *the truth that you* know *that will* make *you free* (John 8:32).

*****

I would be remiss in talking about the Word as final authority without bringing attention to our Mighty King Jesus who is the Word Incarnate. He is the Word become flesh who dwelt among us (John 1:14). Whenever we celebrate the birth of Christ at Christmas, we read about the many magi who traveled from the East bearing gifts for Jesus. These magi were a group of median priests and astronomers who were strongly influenced by Daniel – the same Daniel who served in Babylon during the Israelite captivity.

As the magi entered Jerusalem, they demanded to know: "Where is He? Where is the one born King of the Jews?" This word "king" describes a king, an emperor, or the highest ruler. They were searching for the greatest and highest king to ever be born - the King of all Kings - so that they, as mighty as they were, could bow themselves to the ground before Him in worship and adoration.

History tells us that the magi of the East were exceedingly rich and powerful, even more so than kings! Magi held a very powerful position. In fact, they were considered to be kingmakers. They were known to remove a king or set a king up in one day. Kings were very reverential and even terrified of the magi, who were financially rich political and spiritual leaders, devoted to interpreting dreams and studying the constellations. We have no one in the world today to compare to the magi.

When the magi traveled, they did so in huge caravans with hundreds of servants and bodyguards to protect them - hardly what we see depicted in the traditional Nativity scene! These magi in particular were carrying very costly extravagant gifts for the King of all Kings whom they came to pay homage to. From these men, the Child Jesus received a storehouse of treasures and cargo filled with invaluable resources. Traditionally, the size of diplomatic gifts given to a king was in proportion to the status of that king. Because Christ was of the highest status, they brought Him the greatest gifts of utmost value, enormous gifts fit for the highest rank of nobility.

When Matthew says, **"Behold, there came wisemen from the east to Jerusalem"** (Matthew 2:1), that word "behold" denotes utter wonderment or astonishment to consider. Matthew was awestruck in considering the magi. Since these powerful and influential magi paid such honor and homage to the Greatest

King of all Kings, the Mighty Majestic Lord Jesus Christ, we ought to pay careful attention to Whom we serve.

Isaiah 6:1-4 says, **"In the year that King Uzziah died, I saw the Lord sitting on a throne, high and lifted up, and the train of His robe filled the temple. Above it stood seraphim; each one had six wings: with two he covered his face, and with two he flew. And one cried to another and said: 'Holy, holy, holy is the LORD of hosts; the whole earth is full of His glory!' And the posts of the door were shaken by the voice of him who cried out, and the house was filled with smoke"** (NKJV). In the days of Isaiah, when kings conquered kings, they would cut off a piece of the defeated king's robe and add it to the train of their own robe. That long and glorious robe symbolized the strength and security of the king. The more enemies they subdued and conquered, the longer the train of their robe became. The reason Jesus' train fills the temple is because Jesus has conquered every principality and power, every ruler and dominion, leaving none unconquered.

This Champion Jesus has defeated the devil, taken the keys of death and Hades, and bestowed His mighty authority on us, the Church. Nothing is impossible for Him. The King of Kings is ruling and reigning in and through us, His Body in the earth, the Temple of the Holy Ghost. Through Him we are binding and holding the devil and subduing his evil works by using the authority of Jesus Christ the Anointed One in the earth. We as believers in Christ are literally manifesting the kingdom of God on the earth. Glory and Hallelujah too!

Chapter Eleven

103 Things God Said About Your Authority

"*F*AITH COMES BY HEARING, **and hearing by the word of God**" (Romans 10:17). Therefore I believe that every believer in Christ needs to be taught by the great and mighty Holy Spirit how great our authority is over darkness, demons, death, and every power of the enemy. You can be filled with joy, knowing that this is part of your inheritance.

As you read through these verses about your authority in Christ Jesus, pray, and ask **"that the God of our Lord Jesus Christ, the Father of glory, may give unto you the spirit of wisdom and revelation in the knowledge of him: The** eyes of your understanding being enlightened; that ye may know what is the hope of his calling, and what the riches of the glory of his inheritance in the saints, and what is the exceeding greatness of his power to us-ward who believe, according to the working of his mighty power, which he wrought in Christ, when he raised him from the dead, and set him at his own right hand in the heavenly places, far above all principality, and power, and might, and dominion, and every name that is named, not only in this world, but also in that which is to come: and hath put all things under his feet, and gave him to be the head over all things to the church, which is his body, the fulness of him that filleth all in all" (Ephesians 1:17-23).

1. You are My child. (Galatians 3:26)
2. I have made you alive with Me and have forgiven all of your sin. (Colossians 2:13)
3. You are now the righteousness of God. (2 Corinthians 5:21)
4. You can come boldly to My throne of grace to obtain mercy and find grace to help in time of need. (Hebrews 4:16)
5. You are My ambassador. (2 Corinthians 5:20)
6. I dwell in you and you in Me. Your life is hidden with Christ in Me. (1 John 4:15; Colossians 3:3)
7. Fear not, for I am with you; be not dismayed, for I am your God. I will strengthen you; I will help you; I will

uphold you with the right hand of My righteousness. (Isaiah 41:10)

8. I am with you always. (Matthew 28:20)

9. I am at your right hand; you shall not be moved. (Psalm 16:8)

10. My Name is a strong tower that you can run into and be safe. (Proverbs 18:10)

11. I have redeemed you from the curse of the law, and the Blessing of Abraham is now upon you. (Galatians 3:13-14)

12. I have redeemed your life from destruction. (Psalm 103:4)

13. I have redeemed you from the hand of the enemy. (Psalm 106:10, 107:2)

14. I have made you free from the law of sin and death through the law of My Spirit. (Romans 8:2)

15. You are joined to Me. We are one. (1 Corinthians 6:17)

16. I teach you as One having authority. (Matthew 7:29)

17. All authority in Heaven and on earth has been given to Me, so go and teach all nations, baptizing them in the name of the Father, and of the Son, and of the Holy Spirit. (Matthew 28:18-19)

18. Behold, I give you authority to trample on snakes and scorpions and to overcome all the power of the enemy. Nothing shall by any means harm you. (Luke 10:19)

19. I have given you authority over evil spirits, to cast them out, and to heal all manner of sickness and all manner of disease. (Matthew 10:1; Mark 6:7)

20. Now you go and make disciples of all nations, baptizing them in the name of the Father and of the Son and of the Holy Spirit. Teach them to obey everything I have commanded you. (Matthew 28:19)

21. *You* go into all the world and preach the Gospel. These signs will follow you because you believe: in My Name, *you* will cast out devils; *you* will speak with new tongues; *you* shall take up serpents, and if *you* drink any deadly thing, it shall not hurt you. *You* shall lay hands on the sick, and they shall recover. (Mark 16: 15, 17-18)

22. I am building My Church, and the gates of hell shall not prevail against it. (Matthew 16:18)

23. Don't be intimidated in any way by your enemies. (Philippians 1:28)

24. I have not given you the spirit of fear but of power and of love and of a sound mind. (2 Timothy 1:7)

25. Behold, they shall surely gather together, yet not by Me. Whoever gathers together against you will fall for your sake. (Isaiah 54:15)

26. The enemy may devise his strategy, but it will be thwarted; he may propose his plan, but it will not stand, for I am with you. (Isaiah 8:10)

27. No weapon formed against you shall prosper, and every tongue that rises against you in judgment, you shall

condemn. This is the heritage of My servants, and their righteousness is of Me. (Isaiah 54:17)

28. Be convinced that neither death nor life, neither angels nor demons, neither the present nor the future, nor any powers, neither height nor depth, nor anything else in all creation, will ever be able to separate you from My love. (Romans 8:38-39)

29. I am greater than all, and no one can snatch you out of My hand. (John 10:29)

30. Whatever you bind on earth will be bound in heaven, and whatever you loose on earth will be loosed in heaven. (Matthew 16:19, 18:18)

31. You only need to say to the mountain, "Be lifted up, and be thrown into the sea," and what you say will be done for you if you believe and do not doubt in your heart. (Mark 11:23)

32. Remember that, though you are in the flesh, you do not war after the flesh. (2 Corinthians 10:3)

33. You are not wrestling against flesh and blood, but against principalities, against powers, against the rulers of the darkness of this age, against the spiritual hosts of wickedness in the heavenly places. (Ephesians 6:12)

34. The weapons of your warfare are not carnal, but they are mighty for the pulling down of strongholds. (2 Corinthians 10:4)

35. My angels excel in strength and do My commands. They hearken unto the voice of My Word. (Psalm 103:20)

36. At My Name every knee will bow, and every tongue confess Me as Lord. (Philippians 2:9-11)

37. You will receive power when the Holy Spirit comes upon you, and you will be My witness even to the ends of the earth. (Acts 1:8)

38. You will live in Me by My power. (2 Corinthians 13:4)

39. You are My body and a part of it. (1 Corinthians 12:27)

40. Therefore you are seated with Me at the Father's right hand, far above all principality and power and might and dominion, and every name that is named, not only in this world but also in that which is to come. (Ephesians 1:20-21)

41. All things have been put under your feet because I am the head of the Church, which is My body. (Ephesians 1:22-23)

42. I have raised you up with Me and seated you with Me in heavenly places. (Ephesians 2:6)

43. I have qualified you to be a partaker of My inheritance. (Colossians 1:12)

44. Every place that the sole of your foot shall tread upon, that I have given unto you. (Joshua 1:3)

45. You are more than a conqueror in Me. I love you. (Romans 8:37)

46. I have caused you to triumph in Me. (2 Corinthians 2:14)

47. Stand still and see the salvation of the Lord. (2 Chronicles 20:17)

48. Look up, and lift up your head, for your redemption draweth nigh. (Luke 21:28)

49. As I am, so are you in this world. (1 John 4:17)

50. You were created in My image. (Genesis 1:27; Colossians 3:10)

51. If I am for you, who can be against you? (Romans 8:31)

52. I am on your side. Do not fear. (Psalm 118:6)

53. Be fully persuaded that, what I have promised, I am able also to perform. (Romans 4:21)

54. You have been born of God and have overcome the world through your faith. (1 John 5:4)

55. You are from God and have overcome; I am greater in you than the enemy that is in the world. (1 John 4:4)

56. I will deliver you from every evil work and will preserve you unto My heavenly kingdom. (2 Timothy 4:18)

57. I am able to do exceeding abundantly above all you can ask or think according to the power that works within you. (Ephesians 3:20)

58. Fight the good fight of faith, and hold tightly to the eternal life to which I have called you. (1 Timothy 6:12)

59. Contend for the faith that has been entrusted to you. (Jude 1:3)

60. I tasted death so you don't have to. (Hebrews 2:9)

61. I have abolished, destroyed, and broken the power of death and have illuminated the way to life and immortality through the Good News. (2 Timothy 1:10)

62. I have destroyed him who held the power of death. I have freed you from fear of death (Hebrews 2:14-15)

63. I have the keys of hell and death. (Revelation 1:18)

64. I have destroyed the works of the devil. (1 John 3:8)

65. I have delivered you from the power of darkness and have translated you in to the kingdom of my dear Son. (Colossians 1:13)

66. I have disarmed the principalities and powers and made a public spectacle of them, triumphing over them. (Colossians 2:15)

67. I (the God of peace) will soon crush Satan underneath your feet. (Romans 16:20)

68. It is My will to deliver you from the evil one. (Matthew 6:13)

69. You are My child, and the evil one cannot touch you. (1 John 5:18)

70. When the enemy comes in like a flood, My Spirit will raise up a standard against him. (Isaiah 59:19)

71. The enemy may come at you one way, but he will flee before you seven ways. (Deuteronomy 28:7)

72. Submit to Me; resist the devil, and he will flee from you! (James 4:7)

73. You overcome by My Blood and the word of your testimony. (Revelation 12:11)

74. Put on the whole armor of God so that you can stand against the devil's schemes. (Ephesians 6:11)

75. Be sober and vigilant because your adversary, the devil, walks about like a roaring lion. Resist him steadfast in the faith. (1 Peter 5:8-9)

76. Don't give any place to the devil. (Ephesians 4:27)

77. Don't be overcome by evil, but overcome evil with good. (Romans 12:21)

78. Forgive others so that Satan will not outsmart you. Be familiar with his evil schemes. (2 Corinthians 2:11)

79. You are established and anointed in Me. (2 Corinthians 1:21)

80. Be steadfast, immovable, always abounding in the work of the Lord. Know that your work is not in vain. (1 Corinthians 15:58)

81. You are a chosen generation, a royal priesthood, a holy nation, and special to Me. I have called you out of darkness into My marvelous light. (1 Peter 2:9)

82. *My* throne is forever and ever, and *My* scepter is the scepter of righteousness. (Hebrews 1:8)

83. The whole earth belongs to Me, and you are My heir. (Psalm 24:1; Romans 8:17)

84. You are a king and priest unto Me, and you shall reign on the earth. (Revelation 5:10)

85. I have blessed you with every spiritual blessing in the heavenly places (Ephesians 1:3). This blessing includes My authority.

86. My kingdom is not just a lot of talk; it is living by My power. (1 Corinthians 4:20 NLT)

87. Fear not. It is My good pleasure to give you the kingdom. (Luke 12:32)

88. According to My divine power, I have given you all things that pertain to life and godliness. (1 Peter 1:3)

89. Every place that the sole of your foot shall tread upon, that have I given unto you. (Joshua 1:3)

90. All of My promises are "Yes" and "Amen." (2 Corinthians 1:20)

91. Concerning the works of My hands, command ye Me. (Isaiah 45:11)

92. I am the one who gives power and strength to My people. (Psalm 68:35)

93. Be strong in Me and in the power of My might. (Ephesians 6:10)

94. I am strengthening you; you can do all things through Me. (Philippians 4:13)

95. I want you to understand the incredible greatness of My power for them that believe in Me. It's the same mighty power that raised Christ from the dead and seated Him in the heavenly realms far above any ruler, authority, power or leader or anything else, not only in this world but also in the world to come. (Ephesians 1:19-21)

96. You have received an abundance of grace and the gift of righteousness, and you shall reign in life! (Romans 5:17)

97. You will do greater works than Me because you believe on Me. (John 14:12)

98. If any two of you on earth agree about anything you ask for, it will be done for you. (Matthew 18:19)

99. The kingdom of Heaven suffers violence, and the violent take it by force. (Matthew 11:12)

100. I make your feet like the deer's feet, and I set you upon My high places. I teach your hands to war so you can "bend a bow of bronze." (Psalm 18:33-34)

101. Earnestly contend for the faith. (Jude 1:3)

102. Don't grow weary in well-doing. In due season you will reap if you faint not. (Galatians 6:9)

103. Be of good courage! I have overcome the world. (John 16:33)

CHAPTER TWELVE

FAITH CONFESSIONS

Two thousand years ago, *a* battle was fought and won for all mankind by our Champion, Jesus Christ, the Anointed One. We as believers need to acknowledge and take hold of the spoils Jesus won for us. Remember, we are not necessarily fighting to beat the devil; he is already a defeated foe. The "good fight of faith" is to believe, receive, and confiscate Calvary's spoils. Part of that fight is confessing the Word of God over our lives. These confessions are here that by them you might wage a good warfare and lay hold of that for which Christ Jesus laid hold of you.

Psalm 91

I dwell in the secret place of the Most High, and I abide under the shadow of the Almighty. I will say of the Lord, "He is my refuge and my fortress, my God, and in Him, I will trust."

Surely He will deliver me from the snare of the fowler and from the perilous pestilence. He will cover me with His feathers, and under His wings I will take refuge. His truth is my shield and my buckler.

I will not be afraid of the terror by night, nor of the arrow that flies by day, nor of the pestilence that walks in darkness, nor of the destruction that lays waste at noonday.

A thousand may fall at my side and ten thousand at my right hand, but it will not come near me. Only with my eyes will I look and see the reward of the wicked.

I have made the LORD my refuge and my dwelling place; therefore, no evil shall befall me, nor shall any plague come near my dwelling, for God has given His angels charge over me, to keep me in all my ways. In their hands, they will bear me up; I won't even dash my foot against a stone.

I will tread upon the lion and the cobra. The young lion and the serpent I will trample underfoot.

I set my love upon God; therefore, He will deliver me. He will set me on high because I have known His Name. I will call upon God, and He will answer me. He will be with me in trouble; He will deliver me and honor me. With long life, He will satisfy me and show me His salvation.

*****

The Prayers of Paul

Ephesians 1:16-20 (NKJV)

[I] do not cease to give thanks for you, making mention of you in my prayers:

that the God of our Lord Jesus Christ, the Father of glory, may give to you the spirit of wisdom and revelation in the knowledge of Him,

the eyes of your understanding being enlightened; that you may know what is the hope of His calling, what are the riches of the glory of His inheritance in the saints,

and what [is] the exceeding greatness of His power toward us who believe, according to the working of His mighty power

which He worked in Christ when He raised Him from the dead and seated [Him] at His right hand in the heavenly [places].

Ephesians 3:14-19 (NKJV)

For this reason I bow my knees to the Father of our Lord Jesus Christ,

from whom the whole family in heaven and earth is named,

that He would grant you, according to the riches of His glory, to be strengthened with might through His Spirit in the inner man,

that Christ may dwell in your hearts through faith; that you, being rooted and grounded in love, may be able to comprehend with all the saints what [is] the width and length and depth and height--

to know the love of Christ which passes knowledge; that you may be filled with all the fullness of God.

*****

The Love Chapter

"God is love" (1 John 4:8), and He lives in me. Therefore, I confess over myself 1 Corinthians 13:4-8a (AMPC):

I endure long, and I am patient and kind; I am never envious, nor do I boil over with jealousy. I am not boastful or vainglorious, and I do not display myself haughtily.

I am not conceited (arrogant and inflated with pride). I am not rude (unmannerly), and I do not act unbecomingly.

I do not insist on my own rights or my own way, for I am not self-seeking.

I am not touchy or fretful or resentful.

I take no account of the evil done to me. I pay no attention to a suffered wrong.

I do not rejoice at injustice and unrighteousness, but I rejoice when right and truth prevail.

I bear up under anything and everything that comes.

I am ever ready to believe the best of every person.

My hopes are fadeless under all circumstances, and I endure everything without weakening.

I never fail because the love of God in me never fades out, will never become obsolete, nor will it ever come to an end.

*****

The Armor of God
(Ephesians 6:10-18)

I pick up the **shied of faith**, quenching ALL the fiery darts of the devil and putting them out in Christ Jesus' Name. My faith in God overcomes the world. The Greater One in me puts me over in every situation and circumstance. I talk back to the mountains and move them into the sea of forgetfulness.

I pick up the **sword of the Spirit**, the Word of God, and declare, "Mr. Devil, I'm standing on the Word of God and the promises of God. I'm standing against all your nonsense, pleading the Blood of Christ Jesus to make right what is not right."

I have on the **breastplate of righteousness**. I'm made the righteousness of God in Christ, and the Blood of Jesus cleanses me from all unrighteousness. I believe unto what is right until the wrong is made right. I call those things that be not as though they were.

I put on the **gospel shoes of peace**. I'm lead forth with peace and joy. I proclaim and minister healing, salvation, deliverance, protection, prosperity, and long life everywhere I go, even to all nations. I'm the head and not the tail, above and not beneath. I'm blessed in the city. I'm blessed in the country. I'm blessed at home. I'm blessed at school. I'm blessed at work. I'm blessed at church. I'm blessed on holidays. I'm blessed everywhere I go.

I wear the **belt of truth**. I speak the truth in the Anointed One and His Anointing and lie not. I hold fast to the truth and enjoy liberty. I follow the Spirit of Truth into all truth. I cast down imaginations, strongholds, and every thought contrary to the truth, the Word of God. I'm the healed and live in divine health. I'm the strong, rich, and full, a joint-heir together with Christ Jesus, the possessor of Heaven and Earth, the owner of the cattle on a thousand hills. In Jesus' Name I have all power and authority to rule and reign in life over sickness and disease, poverty and lack, sin and spiritual death. Glory to God!

Most assuredly, I put on the **helmet of salvation.** I declare Jesus Christ is my Lord, my Fortress, and my God in whom I put my trust. I'm born of Love and am walking in it. I cannot fail. No weapon formed against me can prosper and where my feet tread, God goes, the Kingdom grows and becomes. God's angels are in charge over me so no evil can befall me, and no plague can come nigh my dwelling.

I war a good warfare by the prophecies gone on before me. I **pray always with all prayer and supplication in the Spirit**. I fight the good fight of faith because this battle I will always win!

AUTHORITY: A WORD ETYMOLOGY

ONE EFFECTIVE WAY TO STUDY any given topic in the Bible is to do a word analysis. This is called *etymology*, which, simply stated, means the explanation of where a word came from, or the history of a word.[1] For instance, the word *etymology* comes from the Greek word *etymon,* "true meaning of a word," and the Greek word *-logia,* "study, science."[2] Thus, *etymology* is the science or study of the true meaning of a word!

In the *King James Version* of the Bible, as we pursue the topic of this book, we find that there are two Hebrew words that are translated *authority* in the Old Testament and six Greek words that are translated *authority* in the New Testament. These words can be found by using the *Strong's Exhaustive Concordance*[3]. The Greek words can further be studied using such resources as the *Greek-English Lexicon of the New Testament* by Walter Bauer[4] or *The Analytical Lexicon to the Greek New Testament* by William D. Mounce.[5]

Below are listed each Hebrew word associated with the term *authority,* along with the *Strong's* reference number, how it is used in the *King James Bible,* and its definition:

rabah (H7235): to increase (in whatever respect).

The KJV translates *rabah* in the following manner: multiply (74x), increase (40x), much (29x), many (28x), more (12x), great (8x), long (3x), store (2x), exceedingly (2x), greater (2x), abundance (2x), miscellaneous meanings (24x).

Therefore, *rabah* means to be or become great, to multiply or become numerous, to enlarge, increase, or make large.[6]

toqeph (H8633): might or (figuratively) positiveness: -authority, power, strength.

The KJV translates *toqeph* in the following manner: power (1x), strength (1x), authority (1x).

Therefore, *toqeph* means power, strength, or authority.[7]

Below are listed each Greek word associated with the word *authority*, along with the Strong's reference number, how it is used in the *King James Bible*, and its definition:

authenteō (G831): to act of oneself, i.e. (figuratively) dominate: -usurp authority over.

The KJV translates *authenteō* in the following manner: usurp authority over (1x).

Therefore, *authenteō* means to govern or exercise dominion over someone.[8]

dynastēs (G1413): a ruler or officer: -of great authority, mighty, potentate.

The KJV translates *dynastēs* in the following manner: mighty (1x), of great authority (1x), Potentate (1x).

Therefore, *dynastēs* means a high officer or royal minister of great authority.[9]

epitagē (G2003): an injunction or decree; by implication, authoritativeness: -authority, commandment.

The KJV translates *epitagē* in the following manner: commandment (6x), authority (1x).

Therefore, *epitagē* means a mandate or a command.[10]

exousia (G1849): privilege, i.e. (subjectively) force, capacity, competency, freedom, or (objectively) mastery (concretely, magistrate, superhuman, potentate, token of control), delegated influence:—authority, jurisdiction, liberty, power, right, strength.

The KJV translates *exousia* in the following manner: power (69x), authority (29x), right (2x), liberty (1x), jurisdiction (1x), strength (1x).

Therefore, *exousia* means to have power or authority.11

(Also see exousiazō (G1850): to control: -exercise authority upon, bring under the (have) power of.[12])

hyperochē (G5247): prominence, i.e. (figuratively) superiority (in rank or character): -authority, excellency

The KJV translates *hyperochē* in the following manner: excellency (1x), authority (1x).

Therefore, *hyperochē* means elevation, superiority, or excellence.[13]

katexousiázō (G2715): to have (wield) full privilege over: -exercise authority.

The KJV translates *katexousiázō* in the following manner: exercise authority upon (2x).

Therefore, *katexousiázō* means to use authority over someone as in when a ruler exercises his authority.[14]

AUTHORITY SCRIPTURES

ONCE THERE LIVED a homeless man who wandered the streets of a great city, living on whatever scraps of food he could glean from dumpsters. With no home, no shelter, no place he could call his own, he spent his days living under noisy bridges, inside cardboard boxes, and between alleyways. No one knew what misfortune had beset this man that his life would be this way, nor did the man himself know the exact turn of events that brought him to these streets. He only knew of lack, of want, of poverty.

The unfortunate man did not know there was an account in a bank on the other side of the country. This account had his name on it. It had a balance of almost half a million dollars. It had lain dormant, untouched, year after year after year. This account was the inheritance left to him by his grandfather, almost four years ago. Unbeknownst to the man, there was more than enough money to bring him right out of poverty. He did not need to live this way any longer. If only he knew of his inheritance, oh, how different his life would be!

In much the same way, some in the Body of Christ are unaware of the inheritance belonging to them through the death, burial, and resurrection of the Lord Jesus Christ. Many have never read or fully understood Colossians 1:12, which says, **"Giving thanks to the Father who has qualified us to be partakers of the inheritance of the saints in the light"** (NKJV). But there is Good News! We have the Word of God! We have all His promises for every area of our lives, and we know **"All of the promises of God in Him are Yes, and in Him Amen, to the glory of God through us"** (2 Corinthians 1:20 NKJV). If you find a promise in the Word, it's yours! You can "bank" on it!

Take time to study the Scriptures below concerning your authority in Christ Jesus. Meditate on them; let them sink deep into your heart, thinking about what each one means to you personally. As you contemplate each verse, allow the Holy Spirit to minister *this* part of your inheritance to you. Allow God's Word to transform your thinking, and it will transform your life!

Genesis 1:26-31

Genesis 35:11

Exodus 8:23

Leviticus 26:6-12

Deuteronomy 28:7

Joshua 1:3

Judges 8:18

2 Kings 6:8-17

Psalm 8:3-8

Psalm 32:7

Psalm 72:8

Psalm 91:13

Psalm 103:4

Psalm 107:2

Psalm 116

Psalm 118:6

Psalm 144:1

Psalm 149:6

2 Samuel 22:18-20

2 Samuel 22:30

2 Chronicles 20:17-30

Isaiah 14:12-17

Isaiah 41:10

Isaiah 43:1-3

Isaiah 52:6	Luke 10:9
Isaiah 54:14-17	Luke 10:17-20
Isaiah 59:19	Luke 12:32
Isaiah 61:1-2	John 1:4-5
Jeremiah 15:21	John 1:12-13
Joel 2:11	John 8:12
Micah 7:8	John 10:10
Zechariah 9:8	John 14:13-14
Malachi 3:11	John 16:23-24
Matthew 8:23-27	John 16:33
Matthew 8:28-34	Acts 1:8
Matthew 10:1	Acts 4:29-33
Matthew 10:8	Acts 6:8
Matthew 12:22-29	Acts 10:38
Matthew 16:18-19	Acts 16:25-31
Matthew 18:18-19	Acts 19:8-12
Matthew 28:18-20	Acts 19:13-20
Mark 5:30	Acts 26:15-18
Mark 6:7	Acts 27:21-25
Mark 11:22-23	Acts 28:2-5
Mark 16:17-18	Acts 28:8-9
Luke 4:14	Acts 28:30-31
Luke 4:18	Romans 1:16
Luke 4:26-44	Romans 4:17
Luke 8:22-25	Romans 5:17
Luke 8:26-39	Romans 6:14
Luke 9:1-2	Romans 8:2

Romans 8:11

Romans 8:15-16

Romans 8:17

Romans 8:26-28

Romans 8:31-32

Romans 8:35-39

Romans 9:17

Romans 10:8-17

Romans 11:6

Romans 11:29

Romans 12:1-2

Romans 12:6-18

Romans 12:20-21

Romans 13:10, 13-14

Romans 14:17

Romans 15:13

Romans 15:18-19

Romans 16:19-20

1 Corinthians 1:5

1 Corinthians 1:7

1 Corinthians 1:10

1 Corinthians 1:27-31

1 Corinthians 2:4-5

1 Corinthians 2:9-12

1 Corinthians 2:15-16

1 Corinthians 3:21-23

1 Corinthians 4:8

1 Corinthians 4:20

1 Corinthians 5:12-13

1 Corinthians 6:1-4

1 Corinthians 6:14

1 Corinthians 6:19-20

1 Corinthians 9:27

1 Corinthians 12:1-11

1 Corinthians 12:28-31

1 Corinthians 13:4-8

1 Corinthians 14:24-25

1 Corinthians 15:24-27

1 Corinthians 15:34

1 Corinthians 15:57-58

1 Corinthians 16:13-14

2 Corinthians 1:20-21

2 Corinthians 1:24

2 Corinthians 2:14

2 Corinthians 3:17-18

2 Corinthians 4:7

2 Corinthians 4:11

2 Corinthians 4:13-14

2 Corinthians 5:16-20

2 Corinthians 6:16b, 18

2 Corinthians 10:3-6

2 Corinthians 13:1b

Galatians 2:20

Galatians 3:5

Galatians 3:8-9

Galatians 3:11-14

Galatians 3:16

Galatians 3:29

Galatians 5:1

Galatians 5:25

Ephesians 1:3

Ephesians 1:17-23

Ephesians 2:5-6

Ephesians 3: 10

Ephesians 3:14-21

Ephesians 4:27

Ephesians 5:11

Ephesians 5:17-20

Ephesians 6:10-20

Philippians 1:28

Philippians 2:9-11

Philippians 3:10

Philippians 4:13

Philippians 4:19

Colossians 1:11-18

Colossians 2:14-15

1 Thessalonians 1:5

1 Thessalonians 5:5-8

2 Timothy 1:7-10

2 Timothy 1:13-14

2 Timothy 3:5

2 Timothy 4:18

Titus 2:15

Hebrews 1:3-4

Hebrews 1:7-9

Hebrews 2:6-10

Hebrews 2:14-17

Hebrews 3:14-15

Hebrews 4:12-16

Hebrews 10:19

Hebrew 10:22

James 4:7

1 Peter 2:9

1 Peter 4:11

1 Peter 5:6

1 Peter 5:8-9

2 Peter 1:3-4

1 John 3:8

1 John 4:4

1 John 5:4-5

1 John 5:18

Jude 1:3

Revelation 1:6

Revelation 1:18

Revelation 3:20

Revelation 5:10

Revelation 12:10-11

APPENDIX THREE
SPECIFIC SCRIPTURES FOR YOUR LIFE

"I AM MORE AND MORE CONVINCED every day I live that very few who are saved by the grace of God have a right conception of how great their authority is over darkness, demons, death, and every power of the enemy. It is a real joy when we realize our inheritance."[1]

Whatever the battle, whatever the adversity, we can experience **"days of heaven upon the earth"** (Deuteronomy 11:21) when we realize our inheritance in Christ Jesus and make a quality decision to stand in faith on God's promises. His Word is foundational to every victorious outcome.

Categorized below are some areas in which to take your authority. When faced with life's challenges, position yourself on the Word of God, draw a line in the sand, and declare that what God says about your situation *will* come to pass, in Jesus' Name!

Adversity
- Exodus 14:13-14 . . . **And Moses said unto the people, Fear ye not, stand still, and see the salvation of the LORD, which he will shew to you to day: for the**

Egyptians whom ye have seen to day, ye shall see them again no more for ever. The LORD shall fight for you, and ye shall hold your peace.

- John 16:33 . . . These things I have spoken unto you, that in me ye might have peace. In the world ye shall have tribulation: but be of good cheer; I have overcome the world.
- Romans 8:31-32 . . . What shall we then say to these things? If God be for us, who can be against us? He that spared not his own Son, but delivered him up for us all, how shall he not with him also freely give us all things?
- I Corinthians 15:57 . . . But thanks be to God, which giveth us the victory through our Lord Jesus Christ.
- 2 Corinthians 2:14 . . . Now thanks be unto God, which always causeth us to triumph in Christ, and maketh manifest the savour of his knowledge by us in every place.
- Colossians 2:15 . . . And having spoiled principalities and powers, he made a shew of them openly, triumphing over them in it.
- 2 Thessalonians 3:3 . . . But the Lord is faithful, who shall stablish you, and keep you from evil.
- 1 John 5:18 . . . We know that whosoever is born of God sinneth not; but he that is begotten of God keepeth himself, and that wicked one toucheth him not.

- Revelation 5:10 . . . **And hast made us unto our God kings and priests: and we shall reign on the earth.**
- Revelation 12:11 . . . **"And they overcame and conquered him because of the blood of the Lamb and because of the word of their testimony, for they did not love their life and renounce their faith even when faced with death."** (AMPC)
- (cf. Psalm 18:2-3, 91:1-16; Proverbs 11:8, 12:21; Romans 8:35, 37)

See also: Safety

Animals
- Genesis 1:28 . . . **And God blessed them, and God said unto them, Be fruitful, and multiply, and replenish the earth, and subdue it: and have dominion over the fish of the sea, and over the fowl of the air, and over every living thing that moveth upon the earth.**
- Genesis 9:1-2 . . . **And God blessed Noah and his sons, and said unto them, Be fruitful, and multiply, and replenish the earth. And the fear of you and the dread of you shall be upon every beast of the earth, and upon every fowl of the air, upon all that moveth upon the earth, and upon all the fishes of the sea; into your hand are they delivered.**
- Mark 16:17-18 . . . And these signs shall follow them that believe; in my name shall they cast out devils;

they shall speak with new tongues; they shall take up serpents; and if they drink any deadly thing, it shall not hurt them; they shall lay hands on the sick, and they shall recover.

- Luke 10:19 . . . Behold, I give unto you power to tread on serpents and scorpions, and over all the power of the enemy: and nothing shall by any means hurt you.
- Acts 28:3-6 . . . "And when Paul had gathered a bundle of sticks, and laid them on the fire, there came a viper out of the heat, and fastened on his hand. And when the barbarians saw the venomous beast hang on his hand, they said among themselves, No doubt this man is a murderer, whom, though he hath escaped the sea, yet vengeance suffereth not to live. And he shook off the beast into the fire, and felt no harm. Howbeit they looked when he should have swollen, or fallen down dead suddenly: but after they had looked a great while, and saw no harm come to him, they changed their minds, and said that he was a god."
- (cf. Psalm 91; Mark 1:13)
- See also: Nature
- **Attacks**
- Isaiah 8:10 . . . Devise your strategy, but it will be thwarted; propose your plan, but it will not stand, for God is with us. (NIV)

- Isaiah 54:15 . . . **If any nation comes to fight you, it is not because I sent them. Whoever attacks you will go down in defeat.** (NLT)
- Isaiah 54:17 . . . **No weapon that is formed against thee shall prosper; and every tongue that shall rise against thee in judgment thou shalt condemn. This is the heritage of the servants of the LORD, and their righteousness is of me, saith the LORD.**
- 2 Timothy 4:18 . . . **And the Lord shall deliver me from every evil work, and will preserve me unto his heavenly kingdom: to whom be glory for ever and ever. Amen.**
- (cf. 2 Kings 6:14-17)

Bankruptcy

See: Debt/Foreclosure/Legal Issues

Binding and Loosing
- Matthew 16:18-19 . . . **And I say also unto thee, that thou art Peter, and upon this rock I will build my church; and the gates of hell shall not prevail against it. And I will give unto thee the keys of the kingdom of heaven: and whatsoever thou shalt bind on earth shall be bound in heaven: and whatsoever thou shalt loose on earth shall be loosed in heaven.**

- Matthew 18: 18-20 . . . **Verily I say unto you, whatsoever ye shall bind on earth shall be bound in heaven: and whatsoever ye shall loose on earth shall be loosed in heaven.** Again I say unto you, that if two of you shall agree on earth as touching any thing that they shall ask, it shall be done for them of my Father which is in heaven. For where two or three are gathered together in my name, there am I in the midst of them.
- Mark 3:27 . . . **No man can enter into a strong man's house, and spoil his goods, except he will first bind the strong man; and then he will spoil his house.**
- (cf: John 14:12, 20:23)

Children

- Genesis 35:11 . . . **And God said unto him, I [am] God Almighty: be fruitful and multiply; a nation and a company of nations shall be of thee, and kings shall come out of thy loins.**
- Judges 8:18 . . . **Then said he unto Zebah and Zalmunna, What manner of men [were they] whom ye slew at Tabor? And they answered, As thou [art], so [were] they; each one resembled the children of a king.**
- Proverbs 11:21 . . . **Though hand join in hand, the wicked shall not be unpunished: but the seed of the righteous shall be delivered.**
- Isaiah 49:25 . . . **But thus saith the LORD, Even the captives of the mighty shall be taken away, and**

the prey of the terrible shall be delivered: for I will contend with him that contendeth with thee, and I will save thy children.

- Isaiah 54:13-15 . . . And all thy children shall be taught of the LORD; and great shall be the peace of thy children. In righteousness shalt thou be established: thou shalt be far from oppression; for thou shalt not fear: and from terror; for it shall not come near thee.
- Revelation 5:10 . . . And hast made us unto our God kings and priests: and we shall reign on the earth.
- (cf. Psalm 8:2, 112:2, 119:90; Isaiah 8:18, 11:2-5; Luke 2:40; Philippians 1:6)

Death

- Psalm 68:20 . . . God is to us a God of acts of salvation; and to God the Lord belong escapes from death [setting us free]. (AMP)
- Psalm 107:20 . . . He sent out his word and healed them, snatching them from the door of death. (NLT)
- Isaiah 25:8 . . . He will swallow up death in victory; and the Lord GOD will wipe away tears from off all faces; and the rebuke of his people shall he take away from off all the earth: for the LORD hath spoken it.
- Matthew 10:8 . . . Heal the sick, cleanse the lepers, raise the dead, cast out devils: freely ye have received, freely give.

- Romans 1:4 . . . And he was shown to be the Son of God when he was raised from the dead by the power of the Holy Spirit. He is Jesus Christ our Lord. (NLT)
- Romans 8:11 . . . But if the Spirit of him that raised up Jesus from the dead dwell in you, he that raised up Christ from the dead shall also quicken your mortal bodies by his Spirit that dwelleth in you.
- 1 Corinthians 6:14 . . . And God hath both raised up the Lord, and will also raise up us by his own power.
- 1 Corinthians 15:55-57 . . . O death, where is thy sting? O grave, where is thy victory? The sting of death is sin; and the strength of sin is the law. But thanks be to God, which giveth us the victory through our Lord Jesus Christ.
- Ephesians 2:6 . . . For he raised us from the dead along with Christ and seated us with him in the heavenly realms because we are united with Christ Jesus. (NLT)
- 2 Timothy 1:10 . . . And now he has made all of this plain to us by the appearing of Christ Jesus, our Savior. He broke the power of death and illuminated the way to life and immortality through the Good News. (NLT)
- Hebrews 2:9 . . . But we see Jesus, who was made a little lower than the angels for the suffering of death, crowned with glory and honour; that he by the grace of God should taste death for every man.

- Hebrews 2:14-15 . . . **Forasmuch then as the children are partakers of flesh and blood, he also himself likewise took part of the same; that through death he might destroy him that had the power of death, that is, the devil; and deliver them who through fear of death were all their lifetime subject to bondage.**
- (cf. Psalm 23:4; John 5:28-29, 14:12; Romans 6:3-5; Colossians 2:12; Revelation 1:18)

Debt

- Deuteronomy 15:6 . . . **For the LORD thy God blesseth thee, as he promised thee: and thou shalt lend unto many nations, but thou shalt not borrow; and thou shalt reign over many nations, but they shall not reign over thee.**
- Proverbs 22:7 . . . **The rich ruleth over the poor, and the borrower [is] servant to the lender.**
- Isaiah 62:9 . . . **You raised the grain, and you will eat it, praising the LORD. Within the courtyards of the Temple, you yourselves will drink the wine you have pressed.**
- Zechariah 9:8 . . . **Then I will encamp about My house as a guard or a garrison so that none shall march back and forth, and no oppressor or demanding collector shall again overrun them, for now My eyes are upon them. (AMPC)**

- Matthew 6:12 . . . And forgive us our debts, as we forgive our debtors.
- Romans 13:8 . . . **Owe no man any thing, but to love one another: for he that loveth another hath fulfilled the law.**
- Colossians 2:14 . . . **Having canceled and blotted out and wiped away the handwriting of the note (bond) with its legal decrees and demands which was in force and stood against us (hostile to us). This [note with its regulations, decrees, and demands] He set aside and cleared completely out of our way by nailing it to [His] cross.** (AMPC)

See also: Lack/Poverty

Demons
- Leviticus 26:7-8 . . . **And ye shall chase your enemies, and they shall fall before you by the sword. And five of you shall chase an hundred, and an hundred of you shall put ten thousand to flight: and your enemies shall fall before you by the sword.**
- Deuteronomy 28:7 . . . **The LORD shall cause thine enemies that rise up against thee to be smitten before thy face: they shall come out against thee one way, and flee before thee seven ways.**
- 2 Samuel 22:30 . . . **For by thee I have run through a troop: by my God have I leaped over a wall.**

- Psalm 8:2 . . . Out of the mouth of babes and sucklings hast thou ordained strength because of thine enemies, that thou mightest still the enemy and the avenger.
- Psalm 27:1-3 . . . The LORD is my light and my salvation; whom shall I fear? The LORD is the strength of my life; of whom shall I be afraid? When the wicked, even mine enemies and my foes, came upon me to eat up my flesh, they stumbled and fell. Though an host should encamp against me, my heart shall not fear: though war should rise against me, in this will I be confident.
- Psalm 44:5 . . . Through thee will we push down our enemies: through thy name will we tread them under that rise up against us.
- Isaiah 54:14-15 . . . In righteousness shalt thou be established: thou shalt be far from oppression; for thou shalt not fear: and from terror; for it shall not come near thee. Behold, they shall surely gather together, but not by me: whosoever shall gather together against thee shall fall for thy sake.
- Matthew 16:18 . . . And I say also unto thee, that thou art Peter, and upon this rock I will build my church; and the gates of hell shall not prevail against it.
- Romans 8:38-39 . . . And I am convinced that nothing can ever separate us from God's love. Neither death

nor life, neither angels nor demons, neither our fears for today nor our worries about tomorrow--not even the powers of hell can separate us from God's love. No power in the sky above or in the earth below--indeed, nothing in all creation will ever be able to separate us from the love of God that is revealed in Christ Jesus our Lord.

- Philippians 1:28 . . . And in nothing terrified by your adversaries: which is to them an evident token of perdition, but to you of salvation, and that of God.
- Philippians 2:9-11 . . . Wherefore God also hath highly exalted him, and given him a name which is above every name: that at the name of Jesus every knee should bow, of things in heaven, and things in earth, and things under the earth; and that every tongue should confess that Jesus Christ is Lord, to the glory of God the Father.
- Colossians 1:13 . . . Who hath delivered us from the power of darkness, and hath translated us into the kingdom of his dear Son.
- (cf. Proverbs 3:24-26; Isaiah 41:12-13, 59:19; John 1:4-5, 10:10; Acts 8:7, 16:18; Romans 5:17, Romans 8:31; 2 Corinthians 2:14; 1 Peter 5:8-9; Revelation 5:10)

See also: Devils/Evil/Oppression/Principalities and Powers/ Satan/Unclean Spirits

Depression

- Nehemiah 8:10 . . . **The joy of the LORD is your strength.**

- Psalm 42:5-6 **. . . Why art thou cast down, O my soul? And why art thou disquieted in me? Hope thou in God: for I shall yet praise him for the help of his countenance. O my God, my soul is cast down within me: therefore will I remember thee from the land of Jordan, and of the Hermonites, from the hill Mizar.**

- Proverbs 17:22 . . . **A merry heart doeth good like a medicine: but a broken spirit drieth the bones.**

- Isaiah 10:27 . . . **And it shall come to pass in that day, that his burden shall be taken away from off thy shoulder, and his yoke from off thy neck, and the yoke shall be destroyed because of the anointing.**

- Isaiah 52:2 . . . **Shake thyself from the dust; arise, and sit down, O Jerusalem: loose thyself from the bands of thy neck, O captive daughter of Zion.**

- Isaiah 60:1 . . . **Arise [from the depression and prostration in which circumstances have kept you-rise to a new life]! Shine (be radiant with the glory of the Lord), for your light has come, and the glory of the Lord has risen upon you!** (AMP)

- Isaiah 61:3 . . . **To appoint unto them that mourn in Zion, to give unto them beauty for ashes, the oil of joy for mourning, the garment of praise for the spirit of heaviness; that they might be called trees** of righteousness, the planting of the LORD, that he might be glorified.

- Philippians 1:28 . . . Don't be intimidated in any way by your enemies. This will be a sign to them that they are going to be destroyed, but that you are going to be saved, even by God himself. (NLT)
- Philippians 4:4 . . . Rejoice in the Lord always: and again I say, Rejoice.
- James 4:7 . . . Submit yourselves therefore to God. Resist the devil, and he will flee from you.
- (cf. Deuteronomy 28:47-48; Psalm 147:3; Zechariah 9:8; Luke 10:19, 13:16)

See also: Oppression

Destruction

- Job 5:21-22 . . . Thou shalt be hid from the scourge of the tongue: neither shalt thou be afraid of destruction when it cometh. At destruction and famine thou shalt laugh: neither shalt thou be afraid of the beasts of the earth.
- Proverbs 1:33 . . . But whoever listens to me will dwell safely, and will be secure, without fear of evil. (NKJV)
- Isaiah 43:1-2 . . . But now, thus says the LORD, who created you, O Jacob, And He who formed you, O Israel: "Fear not, for I have redeemed you; I have called you by your name; you are Mine. When you pass

through the waters, I will be with you; and through the rivers, they shall not overflow you. When you walk through the fire, you shall not be burned, nor shall the flame scorch you.

Devils

- Matthew 4:24 . . . **And his fame went throughout all Syria: and they brought unto him all sick people that were taken with divers diseases and torments, and those which were possessed with devils, and those which were lunatick, and those that had the palsy; and he healed them.**
- Matthew 8:16 . . . **When the even was come, they brought unto him many that were possessed with devils: and he cast out the spirits with his word, and healed all that were sick:**
- Matthew 10:8 . . . Heal the sick, cleanse the lepers, raise the dead, **cast out devils: freely ye have received, freely give.**
- Mark 1:34 . . . **And he healed many that were sick of divers diseases, and cast out many devils; and suffered not the devils to speak, because they knew him.**
- Mark 16:17-18 . . . **And these signs shall follow them that believe; in my name shall they cast out devils; they shall speak with new tongues; they shall take up serpents; and if they drink any deadly thing, it shall**

not hurt them; they shall lay hands on the sick, and
they shall recover.
- Luke 9:1 . . . Then he called his twelve disciples
together, and gave them power and authority over all
devils, and to cure diseases.

See also: Demons/Evil/Oppression/Principalities and Powers/
Satan/Unclean Spirits

Disaster

See: Destruction

Disease
- Mark 1:34 . . . And he healed many that were sick of
divers diseases, and cast out many devils; and suffered
not the devils to speak, because they knew him.

See also: Sickness

Drought
- 1 Samuel 12:18 . . . So Samuel called unto the LORD;
and the LORD sent thunder and rain that day: and
all the people greatly feared the LORD and Samuel.
- 1 Kings 35-36 . . . When heaven is shut up, and there
is no rain, because they have sinned against thee; if
they pray toward this place, and confess thy name,

and turn from their sin, when thou afflictest them: then hear thou in heaven, and forgive the sin of thy servants, and of thy people Israel, that thou teach them the good way wherein they should walk, and give rain upon thy land, which thou hast given to thy people for an inheritance.

- Job 36:26-28 . . . Behold, God is great, and we know him not, neither can the number of his years be searched out. For he maketh small the drops of water: they pour down rain according to the vapour thereof: which the clouds do drop and distil upon man abundantly.

- Psalm 1:1-3 . . . Blessed is the man that walketh not in the counsel of the ungodly, nor standeth in the way of sinners, nor sitteth in the seat of the scornful. But his delight is in the law of the LORD; and in his law doth he meditate day and night. And he shall be like a tree planted by the rivers of water, that bringeth forth his fruit in his season; his leaf also shall not wither; and whatsoever he doeth shall prosper.

- Jeremiah 17:7-8 . . . Blessed is the man that trusteth in the LORD, and whose hope the LORD is. For he shall be as a tree planted by the waters, and that spreadeth out her roots by the river, and shall not see when heat cometh, but her leaf shall be green; and shall not be careful in the year of drought, neither shall cease from yielding fruit.

- Jeremiah 51:15-16 . . . He hath made the earth by his power, he hath established the world by his wisdom, and hath stretched out the heaven by his understanding. When he uttereth his voice, there is a multitude of waters in the heavens; and he causeth the vapours to ascend from the ends of the earth: he maketh lightnings with rain, and bringeth forth the wind out of his treasures.
- Isaiah 58:11 . . . And the LORD shall guide thee continually, and satisfy thy soul in drought, and make fat thy bones: and thou shalt be like a watered garden, and like a spring of water, whose waters fail not.
- (cf. 1 Kings 17:1)

See also: Weather

Earthquakes
- Psalm 46:2 . . . So we will not fear when earthquakes come and the mountains crumble into the sea. (NLT)

See also: Destruction

Evil
- Psalm 121:7 . . . The LORD shall preserve thee from all evil: he shall preserve thy soul.
- 2 Timothy 4:18 . . . And the Lord shall deliver me from every evil work, and will preserve me unto his

heavenly kingdom: to whom be glory for ever and ever. Amen.

- Romans 12:21 . . . **Be not overcome of evil, but overcome evil with good.**
- (cf. John 10:28-29, 17:15)

See also: Demons/Oppression/Principalities and Powers/Satan

Extortion

- Deuteronomy 15:1-2 . . . **"At the end of every seven years you shall grant a release of debts. And this is the form of the release: Every creditor who has lent anything to his neighbor shall release it; he shall not require it of his neighbor or his brother, because it is called the LORD's release."** (NKLV)
- Zechariah 9:8 . . . **Then I will encamp about My house as a guard or a garrison so that none shall march back and forth, and no oppressor or demanding collector shall again overrun them, for now My eyes are upon them.** (AMPC)

See also: Debt/Legal Issues

Famine

- Psalm 37:19 . . . **They will not be disgraced in hard times; even in famine they will have more than enough.** (NLT)

- Isaiah 60:16 . . . Thou shalt also suck the milk of the Gentiles, and shalt suck the breast of kings: and thou shalt know that I the LORD [am] thy Saviour and thy Redeemer, the mighty One of Jacob.
- Joel 2:24-26 . . . And the floors shall be full of wheat, and the fats shall overflow with wine and oil. And I will restore to you the years that the locust hath eaten, the cankerworm, and the caterpillar, and the palmerworm . . . And ye shall eat in plenty, and be satisfied, and praise the name of the LORD your God, that hath dealt wondrously with you: and my people shall never be ashamed.
- Luke 8:15 . . . And the seeds that fell on the good soil represent honest, good-hearted people who hear God's word, cling to it, and patiently produce a huge harvest. (NLT)
- (cf. Jeremiah 34:17)

See also: Lack/Poverty

Fear
- Psalm 3: 5-6 . . . I laid me down and slept; I awaked; for the LORD sustained me. I will not be afraid of ten thousands of people, that have set themselves against me round about.

- Psalm 27:1 . . . **The LORD is my light and my salvation; whom shall I fear? The LORD is the strength of my life; of whom shall I be afraid?**

- Psalm 46:1-3 . . . **God is our refuge and strength, a very present help in trouble. Therefore will not we fear, though the earth be removed, and though the mountains be carried into the midst of the sea; though the waters thereof roar and be troubled, though the mountains shake with the swelling thereof. Selah.**

- Psalm 56:3-4 . . . **What time I am afraid, I will trust in thee. In God I will praise his word, in God I have put my trust; I will not fear what flesh can do unto me.**

- Psalm 91:5-6 . . . **Thou shalt not be afraid for the terror by night; nor for the arrow that flieth by day; nor for the pestilence that walketh in darkness; nor for the destruction that wasteth at noonday.**

- Psalm 118:6 . . . **The LORD is on my side; I will not fear: what can man do unto me?**

- Proverbs 1:33 . . . **But whoever listens to me will dwell safely, and will be secure, without fear of evil.** (NKJV)

- Proverbs 3:24 . . . **When you lie down, you will not be afraid; when you lie down, your sleep will be sweet.** (AMP)

- Proverbs 3:25-26 . . . **Have no fear of sudden disaster or of the ruin that overtakes the wicked, for the LORD will be at your side and will keep your foot from being snared.** (NIV)

- Proverbs 28:1 . . . **The wicked flee when no man pursueth: but the righteous are bold as a lion.**
- Isaiah 8:11-12 . . . GOD spoke strongly to me, grabbed me with both hands and warned me not to go along with this people. He said: **"Don't be like this people, always afraid somebody is plotting against them. Don't fear what they fear. Don't take on their worries."** (MSG)
- Isaiah 41:10 . . . **Fear thou not; for I am with thee: be not dismayed; for I am thy God: I will strengthen thee; yea, I will help thee; yea, I will uphold thee with the right hand of my righteousness.**
- Isaiah 43:1-3 . . . **But now thus saith the LORD that created thee, O Jacob, and he that formed thee, O Israel, Fear not: for I have redeemed thee, I have called thee by thy name; thou art mine. When thou passest through the waters, I will be with thee; and through the rivers, they shall not overflow thee: when thou walkest through the fire, thou shalt not be burned; neither shall the flame kindle upon thee. For I am the LORD thy God, the Holy One of Israel, thy Saviour.**
- Isaiah 54:14 . . . In righteousness **shalt thou be established: thou shalt be far from oppression; for thou shalt not fear: and from terror; for it shall not come near thee.**
- John 14:1 . . . **Let not your heart be troubled: ye believe in God, believe also in me.**

- Romans 8:15 . . . **For ye have not received the spirit of bondage again to fear; but ye have received the Spirit of adoption, whereby we cry, Abba, Father.**
- 2 Timothy 1:7 . . . **For God hath not given us the spirit of fear; but of power, and of love, and of a sound mind.**
- 1 John 4:18 . . . **There is no fear in love; but perfect love casteth out fear: because fear hath torment. He that feareth is not made perfect in love.**
- (cf. Leviticus 26:6; Deuteronomy 20:1; Job 3:25; Psalm 34:4, 49:5; Luke 12:6-7, 25, 32)

See also: Oppression/Timidity

Foreclosure

- Psalm 25:12-13 . . . Who, then, are those who fear the LORD? He will instruct them in the ways they should choose. They will spend their days in prosperity, and their descendants will inherit the land. (NIV)
- Amos 9:15 . . . **And I will plant them upon their land, and they shall no more be pulled up out of their land which I have given them, saith the LORD thy God.**
- Zechariah 9:8 . . . **Then I will encamp about My house as a guard or a garrison so that none shall march back and forth, and no oppressor or demanding collector shall again overrun them, for now My eyes are upon them.** (AMPC)

See also: Debt/Legal Issues

Insomnia
- Proverbs 3:24 . . . **When you lie down, you will not be afraid; when you lie down, your sleep will be sweet.** (AMP)
- Leviticus 26:6 . . . I will give you peace in the land, and you will be able to sleep with no cause for fear. I will rid the land of wild animals and keep your enemies out of your land. (NLT)

Lack
- Leviticus 26:4-5 . . . **Then I will give you rain in due season, and the land shall yield her increase, and the trees of the field shall yield their fruit. And your threshing shall reach unto the vintage, and the vintage shall reach unto the sowing time: and ye shall eat your bread to the full, and dwell in your land safely.**
- Leviticus 26:10 . . . **You will have such a surplus of crops that you will need to clear out the old grain to make room for the new harvest!** (NLT)
- Psalm 23:1 . . . **The LORD is my shepherd, I lack nothing.** (NIV)
- Psalm 25:12-13 . . . Who, then, are those who fear the LORD? He will instruct them in the ways they should choose. They will spend their days in prosperity, and their descendants will inherit the land. (NIV)

- Psalm 66:2 . . . **We went through fire and flood, but you brought us to a place of great abundance.** (NLT)
- Psalm 115:14 . . . **The LORD shall increase you more and more, you and your children.**
- Psalm 115:16 . . . **The heaven, even the heavens, are the LORD'S: but the earth hath he given to the children of men.**
- Psalm 128:1-2 . . . **Blessed is every one that feareth the LORD; that walketh in his ways. For thou shalt eat the labour of thine hands: happy shalt thou be, and it shall be well with thee.**
- Proverbs 10:22 . . . **The blessing of the LORD, it maketh rich, and he addeth no sorrow with it.**
- Luke 12:32 . . . **Fear not, little flock; for it is your Father's good pleasure to give you the kingdom.**
- Romans 8:31-32 . . . **What shall we then say to these things? If God be for us, who can be against us? He that spared not his own Son, but delivered him up for us all, how shall he not with him also freely give us all things?**
- 2 Corinthians 9:8 . . . **And God is able to make all grace abound toward you; that ye, always having all sufficiency in all things, may abound to every good work:**
- Philippians 4:19 . . . **And my God will liberally supply (fill to the full) your every need according to His riches in glory in Christ Jesus.** (AMPC)

- (cf. Psalm 16:6, 24:1, 31:8; Proverbs 10:22; Matthew 6:25-33; Mark 11:22-24; John 14:12-14)

See also: Debt/Poverty

Legal Issues
- Psalm 5:12 . . . For You, O LORD, will bless the righteous; **with favor You will surround him as with a shield. (NKJV)**
- Psalm 9:3-4 . . . **My enemies retreated; they staggered and died when you appeared. For you have judged in my favor; from your throne you have judged with fairness.**
- Psalm 108:12-13 . . . **Give us aid against the enemy, for human help is worthless. With God we will gain the victory, and he will trample down our enemies. (NIV)**
- Isaiah 41:10-14 . . . **Fear thou not; for I am with thee: be not dismayed; for I am thy God: I will strengthen thee; yea, I will help thee; yea, I will uphold thee with the right hand of my righteousness. Behold, all they that were incensed against thee shall be ashamed and confounded: they shall be as nothing; and they that strive with thee shall perish. Thou shalt seek them, and shalt not find them, even them that contended with thee: they that war against thee shall be as nothing, and as a thing of nought. For I the LORD thy God will hold thy right hand, saying unto thee,**

Fear not; I will help thee. Fear not, thou worm Jacob, and ye men of Israel; I will help thee, saith the LORD, and thy redeemer, the Holy One of Israel.

- Isaiah 54:17 . . . **No weapon that is formed against thee shall prosper; and every tongue that shall rise against thee in judgment thou shalt condemn. This is the heritage of the servants of the LORD, and their righteousness is of me, saith the LORD.**

- Jeremiah 15:21 . . . **And I will deliver thee out of the hand of the wicked, and I will redeem thee out of the hand of the terrible.**

- 2 Corinthians 6:2 . . . For he says, **"In the time of my favor I heard you, and in the day of salvation I helped you." I tell you, now is the time of God's favor, now is the day of salvation.** (NIV)

Life

- Deuteronomy 30:19 . . . I call heaven and earth as witnesses against you today, that I have set before you life and death, the blessing and the curse; therefore, you shall choose life in order that you may live, you and your descendants. (AMP)

Lucifer

- Isaiah 14:12-17 . . . **How art thou fallen from heaven, O Lucifer, son of the morning! How art thou cut down to the ground, which didst weaken the nations!**

For thou hast said in thine heart, I will ascend into heaven, I will exalt my throne above the stars of God: I will sit also upon the mount of the congregation, in the sides of the north: I will ascend above the heights of the clouds; I will be like the most High. Yet thou shalt be brought down to hell, to the sides of the pit. They that see thee shall narrowly look upon thee, and consider thee, saying, Is this the man that made the earth to tremble, that did shake kingdoms; that made the world as a wilderness, and destroyed the cities thereof; that opened not the house of his prisoners?

See also: Demons/Devil/Evil/Oppression/Satan

Nature

- Matthew 21:19-22 . . . **And when he saw a fig tree in the way, he came to it, and found nothing thereon, but leaves only, and said unto it, Let no fruit grow on thee henceforward for ever. And presently the fig tree withered away. And when the disciples saw it, they marveled, saying, how soon is the fig tree withered away! Jesus answered and said unto them, Verily I say unto you, if ye have faith, and doubt not, ye shall not only do this which is done to the fig tree, but also if ye shall say unto this mountain, Be thou removed, and be thou cast into the sea; it shall be done. And all** things, whatsoever ye shall ask in prayer, believing, ye shall receive.

See also: Animals/Weather

Natural Disasters

See: Destruction

Poverty

- Proverbs 25:13 . . . **He himself shall dwell in prosperity, and his descendants shall inherit the earth.** (NKJV)
- Proverbs 10:22 . . . **The blessing of the LORD, it maketh rich, and he addeth no sorrow with it.**
- 2 Corinthians 8:9 . . . **For ye know the grace of our Lord Jesus Christ, that, though he was rich, yet for your sakes he became poor, that ye through his poverty might be rich.**

See also: Debt/Lack

Principalities and Powers

- Ephesians 6:11-13 . . . **Put on the whole armour of God, that ye may be able to stand against the wiles of the devil. For we wrestle not against flesh and blood, but against principalities, against powers, against the rulers of the darkness of this world, against spiritual** wickedness in high places. **Wherefore take unto you the whole armour of God, that ye may be able to withstand in the evil day, and having done all, to stand.**

- Colossians 2:15 . . . **Having disarmed principalities and powers, He made a public spectacle of them, triumphing over them in it.** (NKJV)

See also: Demons/Devil/Evil/Oppression/Satan

Protection

- Genesis 28:15 . . . **And, behold, I am with thee, and will keep thee in all places whither thou goest, and will bring thee again into this land; for I will not leave thee, until I have done that which I have spoken to thee of.**
- Exodus 14:19 . . . **The angel of God, who had been going in front of the camp of Israel, moved and went behind them. The pillar of the cloud moved from in front and stood behind them.** (AMPC)
- Exodus 33:21 . . . **Then the Lord said, "Behold, there is a place beside Me, and you shall stand there on the rock."** (AMPC)
- Job 1:10 . . . **"Have You not put a hedge [of protection] around him and his house and all that he has, on every side? You have blessed the work of his hands [and**

conferred prosperity and happiness upon him], and his possessions have increased in the land." (AMPC)

- Job 11:18-19 . . . **Having hope will give you courage. You will be protected and will rest in safety. You will lie down unafraid, and many will look to you for help.** (NLT)

- Psalm 3:8 . . . **Salvation belongs to the Lord; may Your blessing be upon Your people. Selah.** (AMPC)

- Psalm 5:11-12 . . . **But let all who take refuge and put their trust in You rejoice, let them ever sing for joy; because You cover and shelter them, let those who love Your name be joyful and exult in You. For You, O Lord, bless the righteous man [the one who is in right standing with You]; You surround him with favor as with a shield.** (AMPC)

- Psalm 17:8 . . . **Keep me [in Your affectionate care, protect me] as the apple of Your eye; hide me in the [protective] shadow of Your wings.** (AMPC)

- Psalm 27:1,5 . . . **The Lord is my light and my salvation—whom shall I fear? The Lord is the refuge and fortress of my life—whom shall I dread? For in the day of trouble He will hide me in His shelter; in the secret place of His tent He will hide me; He will lift me up on a rock.** (AMP)

- Psalm 27:11 . . . **Teach me Your way, O Lord, and lead me on a level path because of my enemies [who lie in wait].** (AMP)

- Psalm 31:1-3 . . . **In You, O Lord, I have placed my trust and taken refuge; let me never be ashamed; in Your righteousness rescue me. Incline Your ear to me, deliver me quickly; be my rock of refuge, and a strong fortress to save me. Yes, You are my rock and my fortress; for Your name's sake You will lead me and guide me.** (AMP)

- Psalm 31:19-20 . . . **How great is Your goodness, which You have stored up for those who [reverently] fear You, which You have prepared for those who take refuge in You, before the sons of man! In the secret place of Your presence You hide them from the plots and conspiracies of man; You keep them secretly in a shelter (pavilion) from the strife of tongues.** (AMP)

- Psalm 32:7 . . . **You are my hiding place; You, Lord, protect me from trouble; You surround me with songs and shouts of deliverance. Selah.** (AMP)

- Psalm 34:7 . . . **The angel of the Lord encamps around those who fear Him [with awe-inspired reverence and worship Him with obedience], and He rescues [each of] them.** (AMP)

- Psalm 34:20 . . . For the LORD **protects the bones of the righteous; not one of them is broken!** (NLT)

- Psalm 37:39-40 . . . **But the salvation of the righteous is from the Lord; He is their refuge and stronghold in the time of trouble. The Lord helps them and rescues** them; He rescues them from the wicked and saves them, because they take refuge in Him. (AMP)

- Psalm 46:1 . . . **God is our refuge and strength [mighty and impenetrable], a very present and well-proved help in trouble. (AMP)**
- Psalm 46:7 . . . **The Lord of hosts is with us; the God of Jacob is our stronghold [our refuge, our high tower]. Selah. (AMP)**
- Psalm 57:1 . . . **Be gracious to me, O God, be gracious and merciful to me, for my soul finds shelter and safety in You, and in the shadow of Your wings I will take refuge and be confidently secure until destruction passes by. (AMP)**
- Psalm 61:3-4 . . . **For You have been a shelter and a refuge for me, a strong tower against the enemy. Let me dwell in Your tent forever; let me take refuge in the shelter of Your wings. Selah. (AMP)**
- Psalm 62:7 . . . **On God my salvation and my glory rest; He is my rock of [unyielding] strength, my refuge is in God. (AMP)**
- Psalm 86:7 . . . **In the day of my trouble I will call upon You, for You will answer me. (AMP)**
- Psalm 91 . . . **He who dwells in the shelter of the Most High will remain secure and rest in the shadow of the Almighty [whose power no enemy can withstand]. I will say of the Lord, "He is my refuge and my fortress, my God, in whom I trust [with great confidence, and**

on whom I rely]!" For He will save you from the trap of the fowler, and from the deadly pestilence. He will cover you and completely protect you with His pinions, and under His wings you will find refuge; His faithfulness is a shield and a wall. You will not be afraid of the terror of night, nor of the arrow that flies by day, nor of the pestilence that stalks in darkness, nor of the destruction (sudden death) that lays waste at noon. A thousand may fall at your side and ten thousand at your right hand, but danger will not come near you. You will only [be a spectator as you] look on with your eyes and witness the [divine] repayment of the wicked [as you watch safely from the shelter of the Most High]. Because you have made the Lord, [who is] my refuge, even the Most High, your dwelling place, no evil will befall you, nor will any plague come near your tent. For He will command His angels in regard to you, to protect and defend and guard you in all your ways [of obedience and service]. They will lift you up in their hands, so that you do not [even] strike your foot against a stone. You will tread upon the lion and cobra; the young lion and the serpent you will trample underfoot. "Because he set his love on Me, therefore I will save him; I will set him [securely] on high, because he knows My name [he confidently trusts and relies on Me, knowing I will never abandon him, no, never]. He will call upon Me, and I will answer him; I will be with him in trouble; I will rescue him and honor him. With a long life I will satisfy him and I will let him see My salvation." (AMP)

- Proverbs 18:10 . . . **The name of the Lord is a strong tower; the righteous runs to it and is safe and set on high [far above evil].** (AMP)

- Proverbs 19:23 . . . **The fear of the Lord leads to life, so that one may sleep satisfied, untouched by evil.** (AMP)

- Proverbs 30:5 . . . **Every word of God is tested and refined [like silver]; He is a shield to those who trust and take refuge in Him.** (AMP)

- Isaiah 26:3 . . . **You will keep in perfect and constant peace the one whose mind is steadfast that is, committed and focused on You—in both inclination and character], because he trusts and takes refuge in You [with hope and confident expectation].** (AMP)

- Isaiah 41:10,13 . . . **Do not fear [anything], for I am with you; do not be afraid, for I am your God. I will strengthen you, be assured I will help you; I will certainly take hold of you with My righteous right hand [a hand of justice, of power, of victory, of salvation]. For I the Lord your God keep hold of your right hand; [I am the Lord], Who says to you, "Do not fear, I will help you."** (AMP)

- Isaiah 54:10 . . . **"For the mountains may be removed and the hills may shake, but My loving-kindness will not be removed from you, nor will My covenant of peace be shaken," says the Lord who has compassion on you.** (AMP)

- Isaiah 54:14 . . . **You will be firmly established in righteousness: you will be far from [even the thought of] oppression, for you will not fear, and from terror, for it will not come near you.** (AMP)

- Isaiah 54:17 . . . **"No weapon that is formed against you will succeed; and every tongue that rises against you in judgment you will condemn. This [peace, righteousness, security, and triumph over opposition] is the heritage of the servants of the Lord, and this is their vindication from Me," says the Lord.** (AMP)

- Daniel 3:27 . . . **The satraps, the prefects, the governors and the king's counselors gathered around them and saw that in regard to these men the fire had no effect on their bodies—their hair was not singed, their clothes were not scorched or damaged, even the smell of smoke was not on them.** (AMP)

- Zechariah 2:5 . . . **"For I," declares the Lord, "will be a wall of fire around her [protecting her from enemies], and I will be the glory in her midst."** (AMP)

- Matthew 23:37 . . . **O Jerusalem, Jerusalem, who murders the prophets and stones [to death] those [messengers] who are sent to her [by God]! How often**

I wanted to gather your children together [around Me], as a hen gathers her chicks under her wings, and you were unwilling. (AMP)

- Luke 10:19 . . . Listen carefully: I have given you authority [that you now possess] to tread on serpents and scorpions, and [the ability to exercise authority] over all the power of the enemy (Satan); and nothing will [in any way] harm you. (AMP)

- 2 Thessalonians 3:3 . . . But the Lord is faithful, and He will strengthen you [setting you on a firm foundation] and will protect and guard you from the evil one. (AMP)

- Hebrews 1:14 . . . Are not all the angels ministering spirits sent out [by God] to serve (accompany, protect) those who will inherit salvation? [Of course they are!] (AMP)

- Hebrews 13:5 . . . Let your character [your moral essence, your inner nature] be free from the love of money [shun greed—be financially ethical], being content with what you have; for He has said, "I will never [under any circumstances] desert you [nor give you up nor leave you without support, nor will I in any degree leave you helpless], nor will I forsake or let you down or relax My hold on you [assuredly not]!" (AMP)

- 1 Peter 1:5 . . . Who are being protected and shielded by the power of God through your faith for salvation

that is ready to be revealed [for you] in the last time.
(AMP)
- (cf. Psalm 23:6, 32:10, 37:23, 121:8; Isaiah 51:16; John
10:28-29)

Oppression
- Nehemiah 8:10 . . . **Then he said unto them, Go your
way, eat the fat, and drink the sweet, and send portions
unto them for whom nothing is prepared: for this day
is holy unto our LORD: neither be ye sorry; for the
joy of the LORD is your strength.**
- Psalm 72:4 . . . **He shall judge the poor of the people,
he shall save the children of the needy, and shall break
in pieces the oppressor.**
- Psalm 103:6 . . . **The LORD executeth righteousness
and judgment for all that are oppressed.**
- Isaiah 9:4 . . . **For thou has broken the yoke of his
burden, and the staff of his shoulder, the rod of his
oppressor, as in the day of Midian.**
- Isaiah 10:27 . . . **And it shall come to pass in that
day, that his burden shall be taken away from off thy
shoulder, and his yoke from off thy neck, and the yoke
shall be destroyed because of the anointing.**
- Isaiah 14:2 . . . **And the people shall take them, and
bring them to their place: and the house of Israel shall
possess them in the land of the LORD for servants
and handmaids: and they shall take them captives,**

whose captives they were; and they shall rule over their oppressors.

- Isaiah 52:2 . . . **Shake thyself from the dust; arise, and sit down, O Jerusalem: loose thyself from the bands of thy neck, O captive daughter of Zion.**
- Isaiah 54:14-15 . . . **In righteousness shalt thou be established: thou shalt be far from oppression; for thou shalt not fear: and from terror; for it shall not come near thee. Behold, they shall surely gather together, but not by me: whosoever shall gather together against thee shall fall for thy sake.**
- Zechariah 9:8 . . . **And I will encamp about mine house because of the army, because of him that passeth by, and because of him that returneth: and no oppressor shall pass through them any more: for now have I seen with mine eyes.**
- Philippians 4:6 . . . **Do not fret or have any anxiety about anything, but in every circumstance and in everything, by prayer and petition (definite requests), with thanksgiving, continue to make your wants known to God.** (AMP)
- James 4:7 . . . **Submit yourselves therefore to God. Resist the devil, and he will flee from you.**
- (cf. Matthew 4:24; Luke 10:19, 13:11-16; John 8:12; Acts 26:18)

See also: Demons/Depression/Devil/Evil/Principalities and Powers/Fear

Safety

- Psalm 3:5 . . . **I lay down and slept [safely]; I awakened, for the Lord sustains me.** (AMPC)
- Psalm 4:8 . . . **In peace [and with a tranquil heart] I will both lie down and sleep, For You alone, O Lord, make me dwell in safety and confident trust.** (AMPC)
- Psalm 18:3 . . . I call upon the Lord, who is worthy to be praised; and I am saved from my enemies. (AMPC)
- Psalm 90:1 . . . **Lord, You have been our dwelling place [our refuge, our sanctuary, our stability] in all generations.** (AMP)
- Psalm 94:22 . . . **But the Lord has become my high tower and defense, and my God the rock of my refuge.** (AMP)
- Psalm 119:114 . . . **You are my hiding place and my shield; I wait for Your word.** (AMP)
- Proverbs 14:26 . . . **In the [reverent] fear of the Lord there is strong confidence, and His children will [always] have a place of refuge.** (AMP)
- (cf. Jeremiah 33:15-16)

See also: Protection

Satan

- Luke 10:17-19 . . . **And the seventy returned again with joy, saying, Lord, even the devils are subject unto us through thy name. And he said unto them, I beheld Satan as lightning fall from heaven. Behold, I give unto you power to tread on serpents and scorpions, and over all the power of the enemy: and nothing shall by any means hurt you.**

- John 8:44 . . . **Ye are of your father the devil, and the lusts of your father ye will do. He was a murderer from the beginning, and abode not in the truth, because there is no truth in him. When he speaketh a lie, he speaketh of his own: for he is a liar, and the father of it.**

- John 10:10 . . . **The thief cometh not, but for to steal, and to kill, and to destroy: I am come that they might have life, and that they might have it more abundantly.**

- Acts 10:38 . . . **How God anointed Jesus of Nazareth with the Holy Ghost and with power: who went about doing good, and healing all that were oppressed of the devil; for God was with him.**

- Romans 16:20 . . . **The God of peace will soon crush Satan under your feet. May the grace of our Lord Jesus be with you.** (NLT)

- Ephesians 4:27 . . . **Neither give place to the devil.**

- Ephesians 6:11 . . . **Put on the whole armour of God, that ye may be able to stand against the wiles of the devil.**

- Hebrews 2:14-15 . . . **Because God's children are human beings--made of flesh and blood--the Son also became flesh and blood. For only as a human being could he die, and only by dying could he break the power of the devil, who had the power of death. Only in this way could he set free all who have lived their lives as slaves to the fear of dying.** (NLT)

- James 4:7 . . . **Submit yourselves therefore to God. Resist the devil, and he will flee from you.**

- 1 John 3:8 . . . **For this purpose the Son of God was manifested, that he might destroy the works of the devil.**

- 1 John 5:18 . . . We **know that whosoever is born of God sinneth not; but he that is begotten of God keepeth himself, and that wicked one toucheth him not.**

- Revelation 12:10-11 . . . **And I heard a loud voice saying in heaven, Now is come salvation, and strength, and the kingdom of our God, and the power of his Christ: for the accuser of our brethren is cast down, which accused them before our God day and night. And they overcame him by the blood of the Lamb, and by the word of their testimony; and they loved not their lives unto the death.**

- (cf: Acts 26:15-18)

See also: Demons/Devil/Evil/Lucifer/Oppression

Shame

- Leviticus 26:13 . . . **I am the LORD your God, who brought you out of the land of Egypt so you would no longer be their slaves. I broke the yoke of slavery from your neck so you can walk with your heads held high.** (NLT)
- Job 11:15-19 . . . **You will lift up your face without shame; you will stand firm and without fear. You will surely forget your trouble, recalling it only as waters gone by. Life will be brighter than noonday, and darkness will become like morning. You will be secure, because there is hope; you will look about you and take your rest in safety. You will lie down, with no one to make you afraid, and many will court your favor.** (NIV 1984)
- Psalm 25:3 . . . **No one who hopes in you will ever be put to shame, but shame will come on those who are treacherous without cause.** (NIV)
- Psalm 34:5 . . . **Those who look to him are radiant; their faces are never covered with shame.** (NIV)
- Psalm 71:21 . . . **You will restore me to even greater honor and comfort me once again.** (NLT)
- Isaiah 29:22-23 . . . **That is why the LORD, who redeemed Abraham, says to the people of Israel, "My people will no longer be ashamed or turn pale with fear. For when they see their many children and all**

the blessings I have given them, they will recognize the holiness of the Holy One of Israel. They will stand in awe of the God of Jacob. (NLT)

- Isaiah 50:7 . . . "For the Lord GOD will help Me; therefore I will not be disgraced; therefore I have set My face like a flint, and I know that I will not be ashamed." (NKJV)

- Isaiah 54:4 . . . Fear not; for thou shalt not be ashamed: neither be thou confounded; for thou shalt not be put to shame: for thou shalt forget the shame of thy youth, and shalt not remember the reproach of thy widowhood any more.

- Isaiah 61:7 . . . Instead of your shame you will receive a double portion, and instead of disgrace you will rejoice in your inheritance. And so you will inherit a double portion in your land, and everlasting joy will be yours. (NIV)

- Romans 5:5 . . . And hope maketh not ashamed; because the love of God is shed abroad in our hearts by the Holy Ghost which is given unto us.

- Romans 9:33 . . . As it is written, Behold, I lay in Sion a stumblingstone and rock of offence: and whosoever believeth on him shall not be ashamed.

Sickness

- Exodus 23:25-26 . . . And ye shall serve the LORD your God, and he shall bless thy bread, and thy water; and I will take sickness away from the midst of thee. There shall nothing cast their young, nor be barren, in thy land: the number of thy days I will fulfill.

- Psalm 107:20 . . . **He sent his word, and healed them, and delivered them from their destructions.**

- Isaiah 53:4-5 . . . **Surely he hath borne our griefs, and carried our sorrows: yet we did esteem him stricken, smitten of God, and afflicted. But he was wounded for our transgressions, he was bruised for our iniquities: the chastisement of our peace was upon him; and with his stripes we are healed.**

- Matthew 4:23-24 . . . **And Jesus went about all Galilee, teaching in their synagogues, and preaching the gospel of the kingdom, and healing all manner of sickness and all manner of disease among the people. And his fame went throughout all Syria: and they brought unto him all sick people that were taken with divers diseases and torments, and those which were possessed with devils, and those which were lunatic, and those that had the palsy; and he healed them.**

- Matthew 8:16-17 . . . **When the even was come, they brought unto him many that were possessed with devils: and he cast out the spirits with his word, and healed all that were sick: that it might be fulfilled which was spoken by Esaias the prophet, saying, Himself took our infirmities, and bare our sicknesses.**

- Matthew 10:1, 8 . . . **And when he had called unto him his twelve disciples, he gave them power against** unclean spirits, to cast them out, and to heal all manner of sickness and all manner of disease. "Heal the sick, cleanse the lepers, raise the dead, cast out devils: freely ye have received, freely give."

- Mark 16:18 . . . They shall take up serpents; and if they drink any deadly thing, it shall not hurt them; they shall lay hands on the sick, and they shall recover.

- Acts 10:38 . . . **How God anointed Jesus of Nazareth with the Holy Ghost and with power: who went about doing good, and healing all that were oppressed of the devil; for God was with him.**

- 1 Peter 2:24 . . . **Who his own self bare our sins in his own body on the tree, that we, being dead to sins, should live unto righteousness: by whose stripes ye were healed.**

- (cf. Job 3:25; Isaiah 58:8; Matthew 9:35, 12:15, 14:36, 21:14; Luke 4:40; Acts 8:5-8; I John 1:2; 3 John 2)

See also: Disease

Slander

- Isaiah 54:17 . . . **No weapon that is formed against thee shall prosper; and every tongue that shall rise against thee in judgment thou shalt condemn. This is the heritage of the servants of the LORD, and their righteousness is of me, saith the LORD.**

See also: Legal Issues

Strongholds

- 2 Corinthians 10: 3-5 . . . **For though we walk in the flesh, we do not war after the flesh: (for the weapons of our warfare are not carnal, but mighty through God to the pulling down of strong holds;) casting down imaginations, and every high thing that exalteth itself against the knowledge of God, and bringing into captivity every thought to the obedience of Christ.**

See also: Oppression

Timidity

- Proverbs 28:1 . . . **The wicked flee when no man pursueth: but the righteous are bold as a lion.**
- Matthew 11:12 . . . **And from the days of John the Baptist until now the kingdom of heaven suffereth violence, and the violent take it by force.**
- Acts 4:29-31 . . . **And now, Lord, behold their threatenings: and grant unto thy servants, that with all boldness they may speak thy word, by stretching forth thine hand to heal; and that signs and wonders may be done by the name of thy holy child Jesus. And when they had prayed, the place was shaken where they were assembled together; and they were all filled**

with the Holy Ghost, and they spake the word of God with boldness.

- Acts 14:3 . . . Therefore they stayed there a long time, speaking boldly in the Lord, who was bearing witness to the word of His grace, granting signs and wonders to be done by their hands. (NKJV)

- Acts 18:9-10 . . . One night the Lord spoke to Paul in a vision: "Do not be afraid; keep on speaking, do not be silent. For I am with you, and no one is going to attack and harm you, because I have many people in this city." (NIV)

- Philippians 1:28 . . . Don't be intimidated in any way by your enemies. This will be a sign to them that they are going to be destroyed, but that you are going to be saved, even by God himself. (NLT)

- 2 Timothy 1:7 . . . For God has not given us a spirit of fear and timidity, but of power, love, and self-discipline. (NLT)

- 1 John 4:17 . . . Herein is our love made perfect, that we may have boldness in the day of judgment: because as he is, so are we in this world.

- (cf. Matthew 5:14-16, 10:19)

See also: Fear/Oppression

Tornadoes

- Proverbs 10:25 . . . **As the whirlwind passeth, so is the wicked no more: but the righteous is an everlasting foundation.**

See also: Destruction/Nature/Weather

Tsunamis

See: Destruction/Nature/Weather

Unclean Spirits

- Matthew 10:1 . . . **And when he had called unto him his twelve disciples, he gave them power against unclean spirits, to cast them out, and to heal all manner of sickness and all manner of disease.**
- Mark 1:27 . . . **And they were all amazed, insomuch that they questioned among themselves, saying, What thing is this? What new doctrine is this? For with authority commandeth he even the unclean spirits, and they do obey him.**
- Luke 4:36 . . . **And they were all amazed, and spake among themselves, saying, What a word is this! For with authority and power he commandeth the unclean spirits, and they come out.**
- Luke 6:17-18 . . . **And he came down with them, and stood in the plain, and the company of his disciples,**

and a great multitude of people out of all Judaea
and Jerusalem, and from the sea coast of Tyre and
Sidon, which came to hear him, and to be healed of
their diseases; and they that were vexed with unclean
spirits: and they were healed.

- Acts 5:16 . . . There came also a multitude out of the
cities round about unto Jerusalem, bringing sick folks,
and them which were vexed with unclean spirits: and
they were healed every one.

- (cf: Mark 3:10-12, 5:1-13, 6:7; Acts 8:5-8; Revelation
16:13)

See also: Devils/Demons/Satan/Lucifer

Weather

- 1 Samuel 12:18 . . . **And Elijah the Tishbite, who was
of the inhabitants of Gilead, said unto Ahab, As the
LORD God of Israel liveth, before whom I stand, there
shall not be dew nor rain these years, but according
to my word.**

- 1 Kings 17:1 . . . **Now Elijah the Tishbite, from Tishbe
in Gilead, said to Ahab, "As the LORD, the God of
Israel, lives, whom I serve, there will be neither dew
nor rain in the next few years except at my word."**

- Matthew 8:23-24 . . . **And he saith unto them, Why
are ye fearful, O ye of little faith? Then he arose, and
rebuked the winds and the sea; and there was a great**

calm. But the men marveled, saying, What manner of man is this, that even the winds and the sea obey him!

- Mark 4:39 . . . And he arose, and rebuked the wind, and said unto the sea, Peace, be still. And the wind ceased, and there was a great calm.
- John 10:10 . . . The thief cometh not, but for to steal, and to kill, and to destroy: I am come that they might have life, and that they might have it more abundantly.
- James 5:17-18 . . . Elijah was a man with a nature like ours, and he prayed earnestly that it would not rain; and it did not rain on the land for three years and six months. And he prayed again, and the heaven gave rain, and the earth produced its fruit. (NKJV)
- (cf. Leviticus 26:4; Psalm 91; Jeremiah 10:12-13; Luke 8:23-25; John 14:12; Romans 8:19)

See also: Destruction/Nature

Appendix Four
Helpful Study
Resources

"THIS BOOK OF THE LAW shall not depart from your mouth, but you shall meditate in it day and night, that you may observe to do according to all that is written in it. For then you will make your way prosperous, and then you will have good success" (Joshua 1:8).

Concerning the Scriptures, Proverbs 4:21 encourages us to **"Let them not depart from thine eyes; keep them in the midst of thine heart."** Position yourself, keeping the Word of God in your ears, before your eyes, and in your mouth by availing yourself to these powerful resources. Take notes, use a highlighter, look up passages, and be encouraged as you continue to dig into the Bible concerning your authority in Christ.

Books and CD Series

The Authority of the Believer & How to Use It by Billye Brim

Believer's Authority by Happy Caldwell

Your Spiritual Authority by Charles Capps

Authority of the Believer by Kenneth Copeland

Bible Truths Unmasked by Finis Jennings Dake

God's Plan for Man by Finis Jennings Dake

Perverted Doctrine by Guy Duinick

The Believer's Authority by Kenneth E. Hagin

The Name of Jesus by Kenneth E. Hagin

The Triumphant Church by Kenneth E. Hagin

Taking Your Place in Christ by Mark Hankins

The Power of Identification With Christ by Mark Hankins

The Prevailing Power of the Blood by Mark Hankins

The Wonderful Name of Jesus by E.W. Kenyon

The Authority of the Believer by John A. MacMillan

God's Structure of Authority by Keith Moore

No Place for the Devil by Keith Moore

Stopping the Thief by Keith Moore (week of increase 2018)

Commanding the Supernatural by David O. Oyedepo

Satan Get Lost by David O. Oyedepo

Dream Thieves by Rick Renner

Dressed to Kill by Rick Renner

Living in the Combat Zone by Rick Renner

Seducing Spirits by Rick Renner

Bitten by Devils by Lester Sumrall

Demons and Deliverance by Lester Sumrall

Three Habitations of Devils by Lester Sumrall

The Militant Church by Lester Sumrall

The Believer's Authority: What You Didn't Learn in Church by Andrew Wommack

*****

Links

http://www.awmi.net/reading/
teaching-articles/authority_releases/

https://www.hopefaithprayer.com/books/The_
Authority_of_the_Believer_John_MacMillan.pdf

https://www.livingwordchristiancentre.com/
media-sermons/?seriescategory=79

https://blog.kcm.org/7-facts-about-your-authority-as-a-believer/

Citations

Introduction

1. The Smith Wigglesworth Blog: April 2008. **https:// smithwigglesworth.blogspot.com/2008/04/?m=0**

Chapter Four

2. "G3438 - monē - Strong's Greek Lexicon (KJV)." Blue Letter Bible. Web. 30 Sep, 2020.

Chapter Six

1. "G1544 - ekballō - Strong's Greek Lexicon (KJV)." Blue Letter Bible. Web. 25 Jul, 2017.

Chapter Nine

2. "Etymology." Merriam-Webster.com. Merriam-Webster, n.d. Web. 12 July 2016.
3. "Student Dictionary." Word Central. Meriam-Webster, n.d. Web.
4. Strong, James. Strong's Exhaustive Concordance. Peabody, MA: Hendrickson, 1007. Print.
5. Bauer, Walter. A Greek-English Lexicon of the New Testament. Chicago: U of Chicago, 1952. Print.
6. Mounce, William D. The Analytical Lexicon to the Greek New Testament. Zondervan, 1993.

7. "H7235 - rabah - Strong's Hebrew Lexicon (KJV)." Blue Letter Bible. Web. 1 Sep, 2017.

8. "H8633 - toqeph - Strong's Hebrew Lexicon (KJV)." Blue Letter Bible. Web. 30 Aug, 2017.

9. "G831 - authenteō - Strong's Greek Lexicon (KJV)." Blue Letter Bible. Web. 1 Sep, 2017.

10. "G1413 - dynastēs - Strong's Greek Lexicon (KJV)." Blue Letter Bible. Web. 29 Aug, 2017.

11. "G2003 - epitagē - Strong's Greek Lexicon (KJV)." Blue Letter Bible. Web. 1 Sep, 2017.

12. "G1849 - exousia - Strong's Greek Lexicon (KJV)." Blue Letter Bible. Web. 14 Dec, 2016.

13. "G1850 - exousiazō - Strong's Greek Lexicon (KJV)." Blue Letter Bible. Web. 30 Aug, 2017.

14. "G5247 - hyperochē - Strong's Greek Lexicon (KJV)." Blue Letter Bible. Web. 1 Sep, 2017.

15. "G2715 - katexousiazō - Strong's Greek Lexicon (KJV)." Blue Letter Bible. Web. 30 Aug, 2017.

Chapter Ten
1. "G5281 - hypomonē - Strong's Greek Lexicon (KJV)." Blue Letter Bible. Web. 4 Sep, 2017.

Chapter Twelve
1. Savard, Liberty S. Shattering Your Strongholds. Bridge-Logos Foundation, 2011.

Appendix Three

1. Wigglesworth, Smith. "February 8." Smith Wigglesworth Devotional. New Kensington, PA: Whitaker House, 1999. 74. Print

PRAYER FOR SALVATION

HEAVENLY FATHER, I come to You in the Name of Jesus. Your Word says, **"...whosoever shall call on the name of the Lord shall be saved"** (Acts 2:21). I am calling on You. I pray and ask Jesus to come into my heart and be Lord over my life according to Romans 10:9-10. **"If thou shalt confess with thy mouth the Lord Jesus, and shalt believe in thine heart that God has raised him from the dead, thou shalt be saved."** I do that now. I confess that Jesus Christ is Lord, and I believe in my heart that God raised Him from the dead.

I am now reborn! I am a Christian – a child of Almighty God! I am saved! I am part of the family of God, and my life will never be the same in Jesus' Name!

ABOUT THE AUTHOR

TIMOTHY J. SABO is an alumnus graduate of Rhema Bible Training College in Tulsa, Oklahoma. Author, missionary, and Spirit-filled preacher of the Word, Timothy currently teaches wherever he goes, bringing in piles of Word of Faith materials and building lending libraries in churches, Bible colleges, and wherever the door opens around the world.

Tim and his wife Jamie make their home in Edmonton, Alberta, Canada, with their two daughters, Mercedes and Jewel.